101 *Best*

Home Businesses

Second Edition

DAN RAMSEY

CAREER PRESS

Franklin Lakes, NJ

101 BEST HOME BUSINESSES
Cover design by Tom Phon
Edited by Kristen Mohn
Designed by John J. O'Sullivan
Typeset by Stacey A. Farkas
Printed in the U.S.A. by Book-mart Press

To order this title, please call toll-free 1-800-CAREER-1 (NJ and Canada: 201-848-0310) to order using VISA or MasterCard, or for further information on books from Career Press.

CAREER
PRESS

The Career Press, Inc., 3 Tice Road, PO Box 687,
Franklin Lakes, NJ 07417
www.careerpress.com

Library of Congress Cataloging-in-Publication Data

Ramsey, Dan, 1945-
    101 best home businesses / by Dan Ramsey.—2nd ed.
        p. cm.
    Includes index.
    ISBN 1-56414-531-X (paper)
        1. Home-based businesses—Management. 2. New business enterprises—Management. I. Title: One hundred and one best home businesses. II Title: One hundred one best home businesses. III. Title: Best home businesses. IV. Title.

HD62.38 .R359 2001
658'.041—dc21

00-065104

Have two goals: wisdom—that is, knowing and doing right—and common sense. Don't let them slip away, for they fill you with living energy and are a feather in your cap.

—Proverbs 3:21-22

Acknowledgments

Like life itself, a book requires the contributions of many to make it successful. The writing and revision of a book are no exception. I want to thank the many people who contributed to the development of this book. They include: Katie Goering of American Business Lists; Lori Capps and Roy L. Fietz of the Business Development Center at Southwest Oregon Community College; the Small Business Administration Office of Business Development; Service Corps of Retired Executives; U.S. Department of Commerce, Office of Business Liaison and Minority Business Development Agency; the U.S. Treasury and Internal Revenue Service.

Special thanks to Neil Soderstrom and to the staff of the Cottage Company.

Contents

Part 3: Growing your business

Introduction

Would you like to own one of the more than 17 million home businesses in the U.S.? Gain more control over your income? Work in a comfortable environment? Cut your commute to less than two minutes? Do what you love—and get paid for it? Sure you would!

It's the American dream. People are setting up their own successful cottage companies at a greater rate than ever before. What kind of businesses? You name it. These entrepreneurs are offering services and products to a new world based on common needs rather than common geography. The new businesses are using technology to reach out to a wider world. They are also focusing on the value of service. They are making a good living in or from their home.

So can you.

101 Best Home Businesses—Second Edition is a step-by-step guide to starting and running one of more than 100 proven home businesses—all of which can be launched with as few as 20 hours a week and without a lot of startup cash. The book will motivate you with examples of how others have succeeded with their home business. Most important, it offers specific information and resources for starting and operating a variety of proven home businesses.

The first chapter will help you decide if there is a "best" home business for you and, if so, how to get started.

Chapter 2 will help you plan the success of your cottage company. It will guide you in discovering the best opportunity for your needs. You'll consider what you'll be doing, your startup needs, customers, pricing and profits. Valuable worksheets will guide you through the planning process to help you ensure that you find the home business that best fits your goals.

Chapter 3 introduces you to the numerous opportunities for home-based profits using computers. It tells you how computers and software work for you, how to select a computer (with specific recommendations), how to use the Internet and set up your own Web site, how to set up your e-mail account, and how to profitably use other new technologies.

Chapters 4, 5, and 6 contain individual profiles on 101 different home businesses you will want to consider. Chapter 4 offers 47 home business opportunities based on labor skills. Chapter 5 includes 31 professional or creative opportunities. Chapter 6 offers 23 home business ideas for those who enjoy serving others. Each profile includes concise answers to the seven questions you will consider in Chapter 2:

$ What will I be doing?

$ What will I need to start?

$ Who will my customers be?

$ How much should I charge?

$ How much will I make?

$ How can I get started?

$ How can I use computers to increase profits?

Chapter 7 includes ideas on how to increase your chances of success by tackling financial, marketing, publicity, and tax reduction issues.

At the end of this book are blank worksheets to help you analyze specific home business opportunities, resources, potential customers, pricing, and income and expenses. Additional forms help you track business income and expenses, manage inventory, invoice customers, and make sure cash is flowing in the right direction.

Why am I writing this book? Because I love helping others reach their goals through home businesses. I've written more than 25 books on small business opportunities. Each book was written with the same purpose: to help others discover and reach their goals through knowledge and wisdom. And each book I've written has taught *me* more about how to do so as I interview and learn from others.

I'm president of Ramsey Business Strategies, a consulting service specializing in helping small businesses to grow. From my extensive experience with home-based businesses—and interviews with successful business owners—comes the advice, information, and recommendations in *101 Best Home Businesses, Second Edition.* The first edition has been so successful that Career Press asked me to revise and update it with the latest information on home business opportunities. I especially focused on the vast opportunities that the computer has presented to home-based businesses in the last few years.

By reading this book and considering the small business ideas and advice offered here, you'll be on your way to discovering and developing the home-based business that will be the most suitable for you.

God bless!

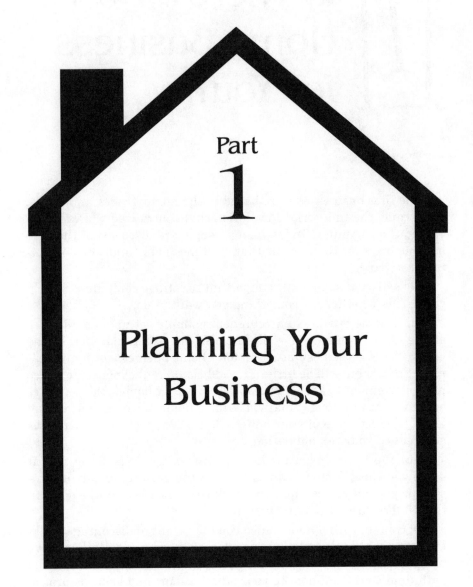

Part

1

Planning Your Business

1 Is There a *Best* Home Business for You?

The first businesses were based in the home: trades and crafts. Then came the Industrial Revolution that centralized work and invented the commute. Today, many people are discovering that the best business for them is one that combines home and work—a cottage company.

Let's discuss some topics important to cottage companies to help you decide whether it's something you want to do.

Most home business entrepreneurs simply set up a small office at the dining table, in a walk-in closet, an extra bedroom, or the garage. This is the best situation for a home business for many reasons. First, there will be little or no additional rent expense. It is also more convenient to keep all business records at home, where they're accessible at any time. Finally, having a home office means you can legally deduct some of your household costs as legitimate expenses and reduce your tax obligation.

But the best reason for having your office at home is that it saves you time. A client can call you in the evening to ask about a specific job and you can quickly check your records or make notes in the job file without leaving your home.

Of course, with a home office you may want to discourage walk-in customers. Don't include your address in your ads. Rather, have prospects call you to set up an appointment. Make sure that the path from your front door to your office is short and looks as professional as possible.

The IRS says you can deduct part of your home expenses for business purposes. A home is defined as a house, apartment, condominium, mobile home, boat, unattached garage, studio, barn, or greenhouse. The IRS says that the physical portion of the home you deduct must be used exclusively and regularly in conducting business. It must be either the principal place of your business, a place where you regularly meet with customers, or a separate structure used in connection with your trade. As you can imagine, there are more specific definitions of "exclusive use," "regular use," and "principal place of business" in IRS Publication 587. I'll tell you how to get this publication free of charge in the mail or online later in this book.

What home business expenses can you deduct and which can you not deduct? In many cases, you can deduct all expenses directly required by the business no matter where it was located. For example, you can deduct the cost of a telephone used exclusively for business calls. In addition, you can deduct a percentage of your indirect housing expenses, depending on how much of your home is used for the business. Indirect expenses include mortgage interest, real estate taxes, insurance, utilities, depreciation, and repairs.

How much you can deduct on the business use of your home depends on how much of your home is used for business. For example, if your home is 1,200 square feet in size and you use 300 square feet or 25 percent of it for your business, you will be able to deduct 25 percent of the indirect expenses of your home.

A word of warning: The home office expense is one of the most abused deductions in the tax system. The IRS looks with scrutiny at tax filings that include this expense. Most are legitimate, but those who pad their home office expense deductions make it difficult for those who honestly use a portion of their home to conduct business.

Finding the best home business for you

What if you don't have much capital or many special skills? Is there a home business for you? Probably. You may have to search a little harder than the Nobel prize-winning-scientist-turned-consultant, but you can find a home business that fits you and your marketplace.

So what's the answer? What type of home businesses are successful? Here are some rules of business I've learned in operating home-based businesses and consulting with others who have done so:

Rule 1: Businesses that require large inventories of products cost too much to start and succeed. So find a business that provides others with service or low-cost products.

Rule 2: People don't buy things that don't give their lives value. You wouldn't buy a TV that didn't work or a book written in Greek (unless you can read Greek). So make sure your business offers your customers a value that is equal to or greater than the price they pay you.

Rule 3: Advertising costs money. So find a business that is so unique that people will tell others about it—word-of-mouth advertising. If it's not a unique business, find a way of making it unique. Add a unique benefit, a special service or a new approach to your business to make it easier to promote and to remember. Keep advertising costs to a minimum.

What I'm describing here is a "cottage company." A cottage company is a home business that profits by adding value to the lives of others. (In fact, the name of one of my home businesses is the Cottage Company.) A cottage company can be operated from a house, apartment, duplex, condominium, or other residential structure.

How can you decide which cottage company will offer you the greatest satisfaction and profit? By considering your abilities and skills in three areas. Answer the following questions by rating yourself from one to 10 (one is low, 10 is high):

Labor and craft skills

___ Are you handy with your hands?

___ Have you made or repaired things?

___ Are you interested in how things work?

___ Are you artistic in any way?

Professional and creative skills

___ Do you enjoy solving puzzles or riddles?

___ Do you easily remember and quote facts?

___ Do you have unique knowledge or training?

___ Do you have resources for specialized knowledge?

___ Are you creative?

Service and social skills

___ Do you like meeting new people?

___ Do you enjoy talking with strangers?

___ Do you like helping others?

___ Do you like to analyze how people think or act?

Also, rate yourself, one to 10, in motivation to start and run a home business. Are you willing to spend many hours planning and promoting your business before you see your first dollar? Is it a service that you will enjoy offering to others? Will you be proud to tell friends what you do?

Rating your skills and motivation in these areas can help you select a cottage company that will give you both personal income and personal satisfaction. It can tell you whether your cottage company should offer physical, intellectual, or social skills—or all three to different degrees.

Chapter 2 offers you more direction on selecting the best business for *you*. Chapter 3 will show you how computers can increase your profits. Chapter 4 will help you apply labor and craft skills and interests to a home business that you can enjoy. Chapter 5 will do the same for professional and creative opportunities and Chapter 6 for service and social skills. Chapter 7 offers numerous sources of valuable help for your cottage business.

8 steps to starting your home business

There are eight proven steps to starting and succeeding with a cottage company you've selected. Here they are:

Step 1: Know your business. Whatever business you select, you must know more about it than do the people you serve. If the business is in a field that is new to you, learn as much as you can. For example, as an auto detailer you must learn about car paints, waxes, finishes, detailing equipment, as well as develop skills that make auto detailing efficient. How can you know your business? Work for or study your competitors. Buy their services and read their ads. Improve on what they do. Ask a librarian for information on trade associations and magazines that serve those in your selected field. Read and learn. The more you know, the more your cottage company will profit.

Step 2: Know your customers. Businesses succeed when they find a need and fill it. That means you must know your customers and what they want. Maybe you've been a customer for this service yourself. What did you expect from it? How would you improve it? If you've not used the service, do you know someone who has? If so, what did they expect? Find out who will buy your service, why, how, when, for how much, and other facts. The more you know about your customers, the more you will sell.

Step 3: Know the law. Business laws promote fair trade and public health. Contact your city and state/provincial government to learn what laws your cottage company is required to follow. Some cities don't allow home businesses, especially if customers come to your home. Most cities require business licenses and other filings. You'll probably need a health license if you prepare or sell food. You'll also have to pay income taxes on the profits of your business. In the United States, start your search by checking the phone book's white pages under "Small Business Development Center." This resource can help you learn the laws for your location and cottage company.

Step 4: Know your assets. You may have more assets to start your cottage company than you realize. Besides your skills, talents, knowledge, experience and some savings, you may have another valuable asset: time. Make a list of these assets, including time available to you. When I started my first home-based writing business many years ago, I wrote each morning before going to work at my regular job. I also wrote during my lunch hour.

Step 5: Add real value. Whatever cottage business you choose to pursue, you must give real value to your service. A secretarial service offers free pick-up and delivery. A pet sitter spends at least one hour each day training the animal in obedience. A bookkeeper prepares tax forms at no extra charge for all clients who have signed an annual contract. Do more than your customers expect—and more than your competitors do—and your cottage company will succeed.

Step 6: Keep good customers. Frankly, some of your customers will be easier to help than others. A few will be very difficult to satisfy. One or two will forget to pay you. Once you've identified which customers are most profitable and most enjoyable to serve, work hard to keep them. Build a friendly relationship with them. Find out if there are related services you can offer them. Find out if their friends and relatives need your services. Keeping and profiting from good customers will help you afford dropping those who aren't so good for your business.

Step 7: Manage money wisely. As money starts coming in from your cottage company, it's easy to forget that it's not all yours. You'll have to share some of it with the telephone company, your supplier, the tax collector, and others. You'll only be able to keep a fraction of every dollar. To keep a larger fraction, you must manage your money wisely by keeping expenses to a minimum while increasing opportunities for income. How? The biggest thief of cottage dollars is impulse buying. You see a product or service advertised that you think you must have to operate. It may be a computer, software, or a special tool. And you may be correct; the expense may bring you many more cottage dollars. Or it may not. To minimize impulse purchases, keep a list of potential purchases with the date on which you will decide. The date should be at least 30 days from when you add it to your list. In the meantime, make a note on the list every time you would have used it if you had it. By the end of the period you'll know whether the purchase will be profitable or not.

Step 8: Do it better. Doing something well isn't good enough anymore. You must do it *better*. You must do it better than competitors do it. And you must do it better than you did it last month. How can you improve your service? By continually improving your knowledge of your business, its customers and the law, by increasing and using your assets, by adding value to your service, by making and keeping good customers, and by managing your money better every day.

Where to find the money you need

A recent survey of small businesses reported the following:

- $ 23 percent had lines of credit.
- $ 7 percent had financial leases.
- $ 14 percent had mortgage loans.
- $ 12 percent had equipment loans.
- $ 25 percent had vehicle loans.

For larger firms, the percentages approximately double in each category.

The ability to get a loan when you need it is as necessary to the operation of your business as is the right equipment. Before a bank or any other lending agency will lend you money, the loan officer must feel satisfied with the answers to these five questions:

1. What sort of person are you, the prospective borrower? In most cases, the character of the borrower comes first. Next is your ability to manage your business.

2. What are you going to do with the money? The answer to this question will determine the type of loan and the duration.

3. When and how do you plan to pay it back? Your lender's judgment of your business ability and the type of loan will be a deciding factor in the answer to this question.

4. Is the cushion in the loan large enough? In other words, does the amount requested make suitable allowance for unexpected developments? The lender decides this question on the basis of your financial statement, which sets forth the condition of your business, and on the collateral pledged.

5. What's the outlook for business in general and for your business in particular?

When you set out to borrow money for your business, it is important to know the kind of money you need from a bank or other lending institution. Let's discuss loans and other types of credit. There are numerous types of loans available, all with their own unique name depending on the lender.

Signature loan. A signature loan holds nothing in collateral except your promise to pay the lender back on terms with which you both agree. If your monetary needs are small, you only need the loan for a short time, your credit rating is excellent, and you're willing to pay a premium interest rate because you're not using physical collateral, a signature or character loan is an easy way to borrow money in a hurry.

Credit cards. Many a small business has found at least some of its funding from the owner's personal credit cards. Computers, printers, books, office supplies, office overhead, and other costs can be covered with your personal credit card. However, interest rates on credit cards are extremely high—sometimes double what you might pay on a collateral loan. But credit cards can offer you quick cash when you need it. If this is an option for you, talk to your credit card representative about raising your credit limit. It will be much easier to do so while you're employed by someone else.

Line of credit. A line of credit is similar to a loan except that you don't borrow it all at once. You get a credit limit, say $20,000, that you can tap anytime you need money for business purposes.

The most common is the revolving line of credit that you can draw from when business is off and pay back when business is good, providing that you don't exceed your limit. A line of credit is an excellent way for a home business to work through the ups and downs of seasonal business. With some restrictions, a line of credit can be established using a portion of your home equity as collateral. Using a secured equity earns you a lower interest rate.

Cosigner loan. A cosigner loan should be one of the most popular loans for small businesses, but many entrepreneurs never consider it. Simply, you find a cosigner or a comaker with good credit or assets who will guarantee the loan with you. If you have a potential investor who believes in your business but doesn't want to put up the cash you need, ask him or her to cosign for a loan with you. Your chances of receiving the loan are much better. Some cosigners will require that you pay them a fee of 1 to 4 percent of the balance or a flat fee. Others will do it out of friendship or the hope of future business from you. In any case, consider this as an excellent source of capital for your new home business.

Equipment leases. If you're purchasing equipment, computers, or other assets for your business, the supplier may loan or lease the equipment to you. This often requires about 25 percent down, so be ready to come up with some cash of your own.

Collateral loan. A collateral loan is one in which some type of asset is put up as collateral; if you don't make payments you will lose the asset. So the lender wants to make sure that the value of the asset exceeds that of the loan, and will usually lend 50 to 75 percent of asset value. A new home business owner often does not have sufficient collateral—real estate or equipment—to secure a collateral loan unless an owner uses personal assets such as a home.

Passbook loan. Sometimes you can get a loan by assigning a savings account to the bank. In such cases, the bank gets an assignment from you and keeps your passbook. If you assign an account in another bank as collateral, the lending bank asks the other bank to mark its records to show that the account is held as collateral.

Life insurance loan. Another kind of collateral is life insurance. Banks will lend up to the cash value of a life insurance policy. You have to assign the policy to the bank. If the policy is on the life of an executive of a small corporation, corporate resolutions must be made authorizing the assignment. Most insurance companies allow you to sign the policy back to the original beneficiary when the assignment to the bank ends. Some people like to use life insurance as collateral rather than borrow directly from insurance companies. One reason is that a bank loan is often more convenient to obtain and may often be obtained at a lower interest rate.

Making sure your business is legal

Depending on the type of home business you start, its size and location, you may need one or more licenses and permits from one or more governments. Some businesses require more licenses than others. I'll talk about general licensing requirements here and in the individual profiles. You should check with local government on other requirements.

Licenses, often a necessary nuisance, give you the right to operate a business as long as you follow the rules. Without them, anyone could set up a business on a street corner and rob customers of thousands of dollars without recourse. Though not perfect, business licensing systems reduce the chances of this happening and attempt to instill trust in buyers. Typically, state, county, or municipal governments issue business licenses. Check your telephone book for government business licensing offices.

In addition to a business license, you may also need to file the name of your business. A fictitious or assumed business name is a name other than the real and true name of each person operating a business. A real and true name becomes an assumed business name with the addition of any words that imply the existence of additional owners. For example, Bob Smith is a real and true name, while Bob Smith Company is an assumed business name.

In many states, an assumed business name is registered with the state's corporate division. Some states will also register your assumed business name with counties in which you do business. Other states require that you do so. In some locations, you must publish a public notice in an area newspaper announcing that you (and any other business principals) are operating under a specific business name.

The typical assumed business name registration requires the business name you wish to assume, the principal place of business, the name of an authorized representative, your SIC (Standard Industrial Classification) code (see Chapter 7 for a detailed explanation of SIC codes), a list of all owners with their signatures, and a list of all counties in which your firm will transact business. Of course, there will also be a registration fee. To help, I'll include the SIC code for many of the business profiles.

Some cottage companies also require professional licenses or permits. These may be required for those who buy, sell, build, or repair houses; those who work with food and those who transport products for others. Your state business office can help you decide whether you need such a license or permit and will tell you how to apply for one. Some professions will also require special insurance or bonding. I'll mention some of them in the profiles.

Your city or town may also have zoning regulations that limit the type of business that operates in a residential area. Most zoning laws simply limit potential traffic in a residential neighborhood. However, others discourage any type of business based in a home. Contact local zoning offices to find out what is allowed and what isn't.

You will have to pay your governments for the privilege of running a cottage company. How much tax, to whom and when depend on what you sell, to whom you sell, how much you profit, whether you have inventory or employees and other factors. You may also be required to collect and pass along sales tax on your product or service.

One more item: Remember that under normal circumstances your home business won't be covered under your homeowner's insurance policy. Inventory you keep in the garage, extra computer equipment, and the safety of customers typically require additional insurance. Once you've decided on your cottage company, talk with your insurance agent about extended coverage. Unless you sell fireworks, the cost shouldn't be too high.

Now that we've discussed what you need to know before you start a home-based business, let's take a look at how to find the *best* home business for you.

How to Find *Your* Best Home Business

Entrepreneurship is the great American dream. Nearly 57 percent of all Americans—and almost two-thirds of those under 30—would rather own their own business than work for someone else. Yet Dun & Bradstreet reports that 28 percent of all new businesses fail within the first three years, and 63 percent fail within six years. The American dream of owning a business can also turn into the American nightmare!

10 steps to success

How can you reach the dream without going through the nightmare? Here are 10 vital steps to finding and making your own business a success.

Step 1. List five things you do best. Include things that others compliment you on or that you especially enjoy doing. Consider trades, skills, hobbies, interests, and activities. Review your life for unfulfilled dreams as well as opportunities for growth. You may enjoy working with flowers, organizing travel excursions, or giving valuable advice to others.

Step 2. List how others would benefit from what you do best. To be profitable, a business must offer valuable products or services to others. For example, if you are good at working with flowers, you can help others grow them, select them, arrange them, sell them, prepare them, or maintain them. In each case, others will benefit from what you do. The more they benefit, the more you will profit.

Step 3. Find out how to give people what they want. Where can you get the tools and materials you will need to help others? If you want to help others with travel, for example, you'll need to learn what travel-related businesses are available, how to find customers, how to find travel resources, and how to make a profit at it. You will want to clearly understand the business's "process," its requirements and its output.

Step 4. Learn the value of your services to others. What are people willing or able to pay for your products or services? If you're not already one, become a customer of the type of business you want to start. That is, if you want to become a computer consultant, come up with a problem you would typically solve and begin interviewing computer consultants on what they do and how much they charge to solve the problem. Also, interview people who might become your customers. Find out what they want and how much they pay for it.

Step 5. Find out who else offers similar services. Every business has competition. Check the local telephone book and national trade magazines to find your potential competitors. If possible, become their customer. Or at least contact them for more information on what they do and how they do it. You should know more about your competitors than your customers do.

Step 6. Learn from the successes of others. You'll quickly identify your most successful competitors. By becoming one of their customers you can learn more about how they started, what they do well, and how well they are doing. Ask your regional reference librarian how to find newspaper and magazine articles about your competitors. Read and learn from their success stories.

Step 7. Learn from the failures of others. As you learn more about your business opportunity, you'll hear about businesses that *didn't* succeed. It may be a childcare service that went belly-up or a consulting service that ran out of clients. In each case, track the owners down and learn from their mistakes. If you can't find the owners, find and talk with the former customers to learn why the business failed.

Step 8. Plan your own success. You know what you want to do, what others are willing to pay for, how to give it to them, and how to avoid failure and ensure success. Pull it all together in your business plan. Write it all down, include financial requirements, resources, estimated income and expenses, and other important facts. Keep adding to and revising your plan until it's the best it can be. Then do it!

Step 9. Make low-cost mistakes. Business mistakes are inevitable. In fact, if you're not making a few mistakes in business, you're not trying hard enough! However, make sure the mistakes you make are *inexpensive* ones and be sure to learn valuable lessons from each one. One floral service operated in a garage until business was sufficiently built to rent a retail store. By then, the owner had made hundreds of small mistakes—and profited from nearly every one of them.

Step 10. Enjoy what you do and how you do it. Life is too short to spend it doing something you don't enjoy, or doing things for the wrong reasons. Frequently, enjoying your business simply requires reducing stressful worry. There's always something to worry about in business, but it doesn't have to stop you from enjoying your enterprise and your life.

Questions to answer

Okay. You've looked at the discovery process. It's now time to consider the questions that all cottage companies must answer:

- $ What will I be doing?
- $ What will I need to start?
- $ Who will my customers be?
- $ How much should I charge?
- $ How much will I make?
- $ How can I get started?
- $ How can I use computers to increase profits?

What will I be doing? Whatever it is, it will be a process! All businesses, large and small, have a process—a series of operations required in making a product or furnishing a service. The process of making a hamburger, for example, requires knowledge (how to prepare), materials (meat, bun, pickle, special sauce), labor (cooking, assembling, packaging), and results in a specific output (a hamburger) in a form that the customer wants.

Think about the processes that you've already participated in. Maybe you've made or sold hamburgers at a fast-food restaurant. Or maybe you've worked in a paper mill, helping process wood chips into paper. You may have experience as a receptionist in a professional office, processing requests into appointments and appointments into billing charges. In each case, you process one thing into another thing that adds value. The more value you add, the more you're paid.

Your Opportunity Worksheet (you'll find a blank one in the Appendix) will help you study the processes that you're already familiar with and what you've learned from them. You'll consider the purpose of each process, its inputs, what you did to add value, the outputs, and who benefited from them enough to exchange money for them.

What will I need to start? There are many things you will need in order to start any cottage company.

$ Knowledge of the product or service you will provide.

$ Skills to add value to the product or service.

$ Resources and equipment to help you add value.

$ People or other businesses who will buy what you produce.

Your Resource Worksheet (see the Appendix) will help you clarify what you already have in the way of knowledge, skills, resources, and potential customers. You can also use it to compare to the requirements for each of the 101 profiles included in this book.

How much money will you need to start your cottage company? Of course, you must know this before you select your business. If you only have a few hundred dollars, you don't want to start a business that requires $20,000 to set up.

To estimate startup costs, you will need to carefully research how much it will cost to set up your business. This includes the cost of preparing and equipping your office, getting required licenses and professional memberships, getting the phone hooked up, and paying for your initial advertising.

Estimating operating costs can be difficult because it requires that you estimate your living expenses as well. Most people who have been employees spend as much as they make. They're not sure exactly how much they *need* to live on. However, by starting with your current net (after taxes) salary, you can roughly calculate whether you require more or less to live on. If you operate your business as a proprietor, your income taxes and self-employment (Social Security) tax will be paid by your business.

Other operating costs are those expenses that you will pay each month to keep the doors open (fixed or overhead expenses) as well as those that increase as sales increase (variable expenses). Expense worksheets are located in the Appendix of this book.

Who will my customers be? Every business, large or small, must have customers—or a market that is interested in the product or service. The lack of customers is probably the greatest reason why businesses fail. You can produce the best products or services, but if there are no customers for them or the customers don't know about your efforts, you will soon be out of business.

The best way to understand your customers is to interview them. Find out what they are thinking. Understand what they want from a product or service such as the one you offer. Ask them what is most important to them. Learn what makes them select one provider over another.

How can you find out what customers want before you start your home business? By interviewing *prospective* customers. Talk with friends who have recently bought or used what you will be selling. In general, you'll learn that your customers want a product or service that gives them a value greater than the cost. You wouldn't buy something for $100 when it's probably only worth $50 to you.

Who will your customers be? That depends on what you're making and selling. Your customers could be individuals, groups, professionals, retail buyers, wholesalers, manufacturers, schools, governments, or others. Your Customer Worksheet (see Appendix) will help you determine what type of customers you prefer and have experience working with. You can then compare these facts to the specific profiles in this book to learn what customers you work best with.

How much should I charge? Establishing your hourly service rate is a simple process of adding overhead and expected profit to the cost of labor. That is, if you want to pay yourself $15 per hour and a benefits package worth $5 per hour, add to this your overhead, say $5 an hour, and your expected profit, such as 20 percent of the labor/benefits/overhead cost—or $5. You come up with a total of $30 per hour. You then apply this hourly rate to the work you do.

Let's look at how many successful businesses price their products and services: The first step is to determine what type of price you will set. That is, are you pricing a product that others will sell to the consumer or are you pricing a service that you sell directly to the user?

A retailer is someone who sells a product to the ultimate or final consumer. The retail price is simply the price at which it is sold to the consumer. A wholesaler is someone who sells the product to the retailer at the wholesale price. A manufacturer is someone who makes the product and sells it to the wholesaler, the retailer, or directly to the consumer.

To set the price of your product or service you need information about the cost of materials, the time required to make the piece, the cost of overhead, and the amount of profit you should reasonably expect. Let's look at these components in brief.

$ **Material cost** is the cost of the materials used directly in the final product. Supplies are usually part of overhead, and not material cost. However, the cost of picking up materials or having them shipped to you is a part of the cost of the materials rather than overhead.

$ **Labor cost** is the cost of work directly applied to making the product or service. Labor not directly applied to making the product is an overhead cost. Labor cost includes both the hourly wage and the cost of any fringe benefits.

$ **Overhead cost** includes all costs other than direct material costs and direct labor. Overhead is the *indirect* cost of making your product. For example, the cost of an office is an overhead expense. Think of material and labor as direct costs (expenses that can be directly tied to the making of a specific product) and overhead as indirect costs (expenses that aren't consumed by making the product or producing the service). If you have purchased this book to make a profit with your product—and I assume you have—the cost of the book is an indirect cost and can be deducted from your taxes as a legitimate business expense. It is a part of your overhead cost.

$ **Profit** is the amount of money you have left over once you've paid all the bills. Many small business owners who have invested hundreds or even thousands of dollars into their equipment and their skills never consider that they should receive a return on that investment. They would never think of renting money to a bank interest-free, but will to their business. A fair profit is vital to the success of your enterprise. Without it, your home business may not be here a year from now.

In addition, you may have different costs for different products or services you offer. The direct and indirect costs for making cakes, for example, may be different than for decorating them. So you should calculate the costs separately.

One popular method of pricing products and services is called *markup*. This term refers to the percentage of the material cost that is added to cover labor and operating expenses. As an example, a cake decorator may add 300 percent of the cost of materials as the cost of labor, another 100 percent for the cost of equipment (oven, pans, supplies, etc.), and another 100 percent for profit. That's a total markup of 500 percent or 5 times the material cost. If the materials for a wedding cake cost $15, the markup is $75 ($15 multiplied by 5) and the total price is $90 ($15 plus $75).

Does that mean the profit on this job is 100 percent? Not at all. It is actually $15 (100 percent times the materials cost of $15) or about 16.66 percent of the total price of $90. The profit is then just over 16 percent. Profit will be covered in more detail later in this chapter.

Another way of looking at markup pricing is to establish a "rule of thumb." In the example of the wedding cake, the rule of thumb is to price the job at six times the material cost (100 percent of materials cost plus 500 percent for markup, which equals 600 percent or six times the materials cost).

Your Price Analysis Worksheet, found in the Appendix of this book, will help you determine your cottage company's hourly rate and per-job rate.

How much will I make? Profit is simply the amount of money you have left over once you've paid all of your expenses. If you have more expenses than income, you have a loss. Pretty simple. Of course, there's much more to profit and loss than numbers on paper. Your business can actually show a profit on paper, yet not have any cash. In fact, many profitable businesses go out of business each year because of negative cash flow.

How can you keep the cash flowing in your home business? By keeping good records, watching expenses and tracking the flow of cash in and out of your business. Your Income and Expense Worksheet (see Appendix) will help you determine how much of the money you make you can keep.

How can I get started? Finally, you'll want specific steps for starting and operating your successful home business. What do you do first? Next? What other things can you do to start your home business on the right foot? I'll tell you in the coming chapters.

I'll also give you a "secret" code for many of these cottage companies: the Standard Industrial Classification (SIC) code. I've included the SIC code in the profiles of those occupations that have a code (many don't). You can use it to find customers, competitors, and marketing opportunities. You'll also use this code as you complete *Schedule C* of your IRS *Form 1040* for taxes. I'll tell you more about SIC codes in Chapter 7.

How can I use computers to increase profits? Let's face it: Computers are here to stay. Like them or not, they are valuable tools that can find customers, manage products and services, track income and expenses, and open dozens of new opportunities for your home business. So, no matter what your experience—or inexperience—with computers, you must know how to use them to increase profits. Your competitors do!

Computers are simply tools that can do mundane work—add and subtract, write and read, and store information—faster and easier than people can. As efficient tools, they can free you up to do more creative work. Computer software today can manage projects, maintain bank accounts, make writing and marketing easier, and perform many other tasks. They can also take you to the new world of the Internet where millions of dollars of products and services are bought and sold each day, much of it by home-based businesses. The following chapters will give you specifics of using computers to increase profits for each of the 101 best home businesses.

A successful home-based business, like any other business, requires careful planning. Just as you wouldn't travel to an unfamiliar destination without a road map, you can't meet your business goals without a carefully planned approach. As you consider a home-based business, give plenty of thought to the six questions and their answers in each of the profiles. This will help you determine if a particular opportunity is the right one for you. Now let's move on to the specific home business profiles.

3 How Computers Can Increase Your Profits

Garden trowels are handy tools for planting and weeding. But imagine the task of digging a big hole in the ground with a garden trowel. It can be done, but it will take many days.

Of course, for digging big holes you need a shovel or, better, a backhoe. Digging the same hole with a backhoe can take less than an hour.

Think of a computer as an electronic "backhoe." It can process data and information at lightning speed. Enter an expense into a program and it instantly recalculates and displays profit. Touch a key and it checks a document for spelling errors. Open a program and it quickly starts a conversation with another computer on the other side of the room or the world.

There are hundreds of ways that you can put computers to work toward increasing home business profits. This chapter shows you how to select computer hardware and software that will increase your home business profits. It will describe the opportunities available to you on the Internet for researching, buying, and selling. It will even show you how to set up and run your own profitable Web site and introduce you to those who have. Finally, you'll see how other technologies can increase your home business profits.

Sound exciting?

A note: Maybe you've already dabbled into computers, software, and the Internet. Even so, keep reading. You will find numerous tips and techniques for applying new ideas within this chapter.

Let's get started.

About Computers and Hardware

Personal computers, or PCs, haven't been around very long in the scheme of things. Though universities and big businesses have been using computers for about four decades, the personal or desktop computer is less than 20 years old. And the Internet is much younger than that.

So what is a computer? It is a machine. This machine is made to follow instructions given to it. The instructions tell it what to do with provided information. The machine is the hardware. The instructions are the software. The information is the data. That's a computer in a nutshell.

For example, a PC has software installed that will format or process words. The software is called a word processor. The data is the words that you type on your computer's keyboard. The software can select the size of the letters, width of the lines, spacing between lines, count the words, change the font or look of the letters, and even check spelling against a dictionary (also software). It can even help you edit for proper grammar. Actually, all it's doing is following instructions previously written by a programmer.

The PC may take up a couple of cubic feet on your desk, but the brain of the computer is a small chip inside (smaller than a cracker) called a central processing unit, or CPU. Everything else inside your computer helps the CPU get the job done. The keyboard and mouse are input tools. So is the CD-ROM. The monitor that displays text is an output. So is the printer. The modem hardware that gets you on to the Internet is an input/output, or I/O tool. The hard drive is a storage tool because it stores both the software and your data. The random access memory, or RAM, is a temporary "workbench" where the software works on the data.

There's one more critical piece to the computer puzzle: The operating system, or OS. You've probably heard of Windows, Macintosh, Linux, and maybe a few other OS. The OS is software that translates between application software (word processors, for example) and the computer's hardware. The critical thing to remember is that application software (apps) written for Microsoft Windows OS won't work on other OS machines. So you must buy application software designed for the OS. But note that Microsoft offers versions of their software for the Macintosh and that many Mac programs have Windows versions.

See, you're already getting into computer lingo!

Want some more? Let's take a look at an advertisement for a PC and figure out what it's saying:

Operating System: Microsoft Windows 2000 (operating system that translates apps to the hardware).

CPU: AMD K6-2 500MHZ (brand, model, and speed of CPU).

CACHE: 512KB L2 Pipeline Burst (cache is storage to speed up reading and writing data).

RAM: 64MB (Max: 512MB) (random access memory included and the maximum you can install).

Hard Drive: 10GB (size of storage area: 10 gigabytes, 10 billion bytes).

Floppy: Standard 3.5" 1.44MB (portable storage disk for installing software and saving data).

CD: 40X Max (40X is the maximum reading speed; a CD holds 680 MB of data).

Modem: 56K ITU .90 (56K or 56,000 bits per second is the fastest speed).

Sound: ESS Allegro PCI (a sound card translates files into sounds).

Expansion Slots: 3 PCI Available (three slots available for adding other hardware).

Ports: 2 USB, 1 Serial, 1 Parallel, 2 RJ-11, Mouse and Keyboard, Monitor (ports are used to connect to other hardware such as printer, scanner, and mouse).

Mouse: Internet Scroll.

Keyboard: Internet Keyboard.

It's probably starting to get confusing. I think it's intended to be so. Consider this: A computer and related software are simply tools, as are dishwashers, saws, cars, and books. You learn about them as you use them. And you don't buy them until you know how you will use them. So, as you learn more about computer technology and its tools, think about how you can apply these tools.

As a rule of thumb, you will select computer technology tools by first selecting the software that fits the solution, then choosing the OS and hardware required by the software.

Useful Software

Now that you understand the basics of computers, you can better see how computer programs or software work for you. And even though computer hardware is discussed first, you will probably select the software tools before you choose the computer and OS to run it on.

Useful software includes drawing, writing, accounting, and database programs. Following is a quick overview of each. Visit a local computer store and read computer magazines for more information.

Word Processor

If you write a business plan, send a letter to prospects or customers, write an advertisement, or write to suppliers, you may want a word processor software program. Word processors simply process words. That is, they let you type words into the computer, move them around, insert words, take some out, and make any changes before you print them on paper. I've used word processors for more than 15 years and would never go back to typewriters. Word processors let you change your mind.

Common word processing programs include Microsoft Word, Corel WordPerfect, and Lotus WordPro. At one time there were many more, but the acceptance of Microsoft Word by business has made it a standard.

Accounting

To track your business's expenses, use one of the popular accounting programs such as Microsoft Money, Intuit Quicken and its big brother QuickBooks, and Peachtree Complete Accounting. These and other programs replace your check register. In fact, they also can be used to print your checks. When entering a check you also enter the income or expense category. It's a little more work than simply writing in a paper checkbook, but it pays off. Reconciling a bank statement—typically a frustrating and time-consuming job when done manually—takes just a few minutes each month. In addition, income taxes are more simple to calculate from easy-to-run reports. In fact, income tax software can import data from these checking programs, saving you even more time.

Carefully setting up your income and expense categories and entering each transaction will give you accurate reports and easier taxes. It can also give you a better understanding of where your profits (or losses) are coming from.

In addition to checking software, spreadsheet software can be useful to your home business. A spreadsheet arranges numbers into useable form. It's named after the wide multicolumnar sheets that accountants use to make journal entries. There are many ways you can use spreadsheet programs.

As an example, a basic spreadsheet program (available for less than $100) lets you enter horizontal rows of job expense categories and vertical columns of numbers in cells. Most important, you can then instruct the program to make calculations on any or all of the cells and it will do so in less than a second. And if you update a number, the program automatically recalculates the totals for you. Many spreadsheet programs can follow instructions you write, called *macros*, to do special calculations automatically. For example, a macro can select all of the invoices over 60 days due and total them up, or give you the percentage of their total versus all invoices. Better spreadsheets will also produce fancy graphs and pie charts that make reports easier to understand. They impress lenders and other financial types, too.

Popular spreadsheet programs include Microsoft Excel, Lotus 1-2-3, and Corel Quattro Pro.

Database

Why would a home business ever need database software? A database is much like an index card file box. You can store thousands of pieces of information. But a database program is even better than a file box because it finds information in the files in a fraction of a second.

The most common application of a database program for a home business is inventory. You can use a database to keep track of stock as you buy it, what you paid for it, and how it was used. You can link the database to a spreadsheet to determine if the stock was profitable. In addition, a database is useful for keeping track of customers, suppliers, and other resources.

The most popular database programs include Microsoft Access, Lotus Approach, and FileMaker.

CAD

There are many useful computer-aided drafting, or CAD, software programs available today. They are quite useful for drawing project plans. All require either a mouse or a drawing pad for input.

The drawing tool is used to draw lines and shapes, move objects, identify components, and even add colors to the drawing.

Popular entry-level CAD programs include Autodesk AutoCAD LT and Autodesk QuickCAD. Microsoft Visio is a drawing and diagramming program.

Integrated Programs

Fortunately, you can also find integrated software programs that combine the primary programs: word processor, spreadsheet, and database. Some packages include other related programs such as Internet browsers. One advantage of integrated software is that they operate similarly so once you learn one you're halfway to learning the others. As important, integrated packages are less expensive than individual programs.

For example, Microsoft Works Suite is an inexpensive (about $100) package that includes integrated word processor, spreadsheet, database, and other tools. For bigger business, Microsoft Office includes more robust tools for $300 to $600 plus. Corel WordPerfect Office includes a similar package.

Other Programs

Computer software tools have been written to solve many small business problems. For example, desktop publishing software (Adobe PageMaker, Microsoft Publisher, Quark Xpress, Corel Ventura) help publish documents, magazines, and books (like this one). Graphic programs (Adobe Illustrator, Corel Draw) are use for drawing. Presentation software (Microsoft Powerpoint, Corel Presentations) simplifies developing business presentations to clients and lenders. Project management software (Microsoft Project) helps plan and track complex projects. Contact management software (Interact ACT!) helps manage business relationships.

There are others. You'll learn about them as you enter and explore the world of computer technology, applying what you learn to your home business. Chapters 4, 5, and 6 of this book ask and answer seven questions about each home business opportunity including "How can I use computers to increase profits?".

Using the Internet

So what's all this talk about the "Internet"? And how can the Internet make my home business more profitable and enjoyable?

Good questions!

The Internet is an inter-network of computers that use telephone lines to "talk" (share data) with each other. Using hardware called *modems* (*mo*dulator-*dem*odulators), computers establish connections with other computers (per your instructions), then send and receive data. If the data is in the form called hyper-text markup language (HTML), the results are graphic with formatted text, images, and other useful structure. The HTML is read and translated by a *browser* software program (Netscape Communicator, Microsoft Explorer) and displayed on the computer screen.

Internet web pages include links, specially formatted words and phrases that, when selected, automatically load another web page. For example, from the CNN Web page (*www.cnn.com*), you can select a story headline and the link will load the page with the story's full text.

So what?

Imagine life without telephones. You couldn't call suppliers and order materials, customers couldn't call you to order your products, you couldn't talk with friends. Computers use the telephone system in the same way. Using the Internet you can research materials, order supplies, track shipments, show others what your products look like, take orders for your product or service, and even do your banking "online."

Certainly you can run your home business without the Internet—and without a telephone. But just as the telephone extends the field of potential customers, so will the Internet. Even if you don't want to mess with setting up a Web site and photographing and selling your products, you can still use the Internet for research and for buying.

Fortunately, you don't need to buy a computer and software to get on the Internet. In most communities, libraries or other public resources (colleges, government services) have computers with Internet access for use by the public. If local libraries don't offer access, take a computer or other course at a community college and you can typically use their computer lab. Many communities have Internet cafés or bookstores with Internet access for a small fee. Other communities have copy shops that have fee-based computer rentals. Some large computer stores do the same. Check around!

Once on the Internet you can easily find information using one of the many search engines:

$ Yahoo: *www.yahoo.com*

$ Lycos: *www.lycos.com*

$ HotBot: *www.hotbot.com*

$ Looksmart: *www.looksmart.com*

$ Northern Light: *www.northernlight.com*

Simply enter a word or phrase in the SEARCH field on these pages and press enter. For example, searching for "home business" on Lycos found 349 categories and 15,648,306 sites about the topic. Read the "Search Tips" on the page to learn how to narrow down the search.

Setting Up Your Web site

Okay, maybe you've already visited the wonder world of "dub-dub-dub" (www or double-u, double-u, double-u), also known as "the Web." And maybe you've decided that you want to sell your products or services over the Internet. How can you get started?

First, get on the Internet as a consumer. Either through a local library, a friend's computer, one at work, or your own, take a look at the Internet and what it's about. If you have a computer with a modem, you can contact a local or national Internet Service Provider (ISP). America Online, for example, is a national ISP. Pacific Net is a local ISP that accesses the Internet much like a local telephone service lets you call long distance. The cost varies but is typically $15 to $30 a month plus the computer. Make sure your ISP offers a local access telephone number so you're not paying long-distance charges every time you "log on."

You're on. Start looking around for other home businesses that are already online. You'll quickly learn who's doing what—and how. Keep notes. Save the URL (uniform resource locator) addresses, such as *www.careerpress.com*, using the Bookmark feature of your browser software.

More terminology. The URL *www.careerpress.com* includes a domain name: careerpress.com. How do you get one of these for yourself? Maybe you want one like superduperhomebusiness.com. Then potential customers can enter your domain name in their browser and quickly access your new Web site. There are many businesses that offer domain name registration. The best place to start is with your ISP. They can check out available names, make suggestions, and show you how to "park" your registered domain until you're ready to use it.

In fact, your ISP probably offers different packages for individuals and small businesses that include Web hosting, storage, e-mail addresses, and other services.

How can people buy things over the Internet? Through what are called "secure servers." A *server* is a computer that's always on and can be accessed through the Internet. A *secure server* is one that includes software to encrypt sensitive information such as credit card numbers. It must work because billions of dollars of goods and services are sold over the Internet each year and fraud level is no more than through traditional businesses.

So whichever ISP you use for selling your products or services, it will require a secure server and related software. Many ISPs offer packages specifically designed for Internet sales. In fact, you can have them or one of their contractors even design your Web site, set up order-taking, and automatically deposit money in your bank account. Really!

Knowledge is power. Unless you're experienced with Internet buying and selling, either take some time to learn about it or hire someone who already does. Although hiring a contractor or service is the quickest path, it is also the most expensive. Consider doing it yourself. There are excellent books available on the topic of setting up an Internet site.

An alternative to all of this is to link up with other home businesses in your area or your field and cooperatively market your products on the Internet. It's cheaper than going it alone. But be careful of what you're agreeing to do and pay. Partnerships can make business twice as easy or twice as difficult.

Let's walk through an example home business Web site to see how things happen. The customer uses a search engine (Yahoo, Looksmart, etc.) to search for "Dan Ramsey." The search returns 520 entries with the word somewhere on the Web site, ranked by density (how many times the word occurs). One of the highest listings is for "Mulligan Press" so the customer selects (clicks on) the link which automatically takes him to *www.mulliganpress.com.*

Mulligan Press's Web site includes an introduction, descriptions and photographs of products, as well as pricing and ordering information. Selecting a specific book, a new Web page appears with the image of a lock at the top of the page indicating a secure page. The customer enters a shipping address and a credit card number and expiration date, then selects "Order."

Behind the scenes, the credit card data is encrypted and sent by a telephone data line to the card authorization company who reviews it and approves or rejects it within seconds. A "Thank You for Your Order" page appears and the customer goes on his way.

In most cases, an order confirmation is automatically e-mailed to the customer within minutes, confirming product, price, and charge. Another automatic e-mail message is typically sent when the product is shipped to the customer.

Of course, there's much more to setting up a reliable Web site to sell your products or services. That's why it's recommended that you get help through an ISP or a Web sales specialist.

Is a Web site profitable? It depends. The advantage of a Web site for selling your products or services is that you can now potentially sell to millions of folks who use and buy over the Internet. However, it takes more business and computer skills—and more money—than setting up a table at a craft fair that hundreds will visit. So it's not an easy decision to make. But it can be done. Thousands of small businesses are conducting profitable businesses on the Internet. So can you!

Setting Up Your E-mail Account

E-mail is electronic mail. It's probably the major reason why people get on the Internet. With an Internet e-mail account from your ISP and e-mail software (built in to most browser programs) you can send e-mail to customers, friends, suppliers, and others around the world. An e-mail address is easily recognizable as it has an "at" sign — @ — within in. For example, dan@mulliganpress.com is one of my e-mail accounts (I have five for business, personal, and hobby use).

An e-mail account can be ordered from your local ISP or from one of the national ISPs such as America Online (AOL). Free e-mail accounts are available from sources like *www.hotmail.com*, but there is typically a string attached. A one-line advertisement for HotMail appears at the bottom of every message you send.

Other Profitable Technology

There are a couple of other fields where computer technology benefits home-based businesses. The technology is digital.

Compact Disks, or CDs, are used to save and view data. The data can be a multimedia training course on using a new software program, it can be the entire contents of a book on a single CD, or it can be the music you enjoy while you're working.

Another valuable digital technology that home businesses can use is digital photography. Traditional photography uses light and chemistry to impregnate special paper with images that can be processed into photographs. Digital photography uses light-sensitive components to read an image as digits that can be displayed and printed by a computer.

Besides being fun, digital photography is useful. Digital photographs of your products and processes can be edited on a computer, then printed or uploaded to the Internet. You can take a photograph of your latest project and have it up on the Internet for the world to see within just a few minutes. Amazing!

There are many applications for digital photography. But you'll need a new tool: a digital camera. They cost from $200 to more than $1,000 for consumer-level cameras. The quality of a camera is measured by the resolution, or number of dots per inch (dpi). For example, a basic digital camera may have a resolution of 640 x 480 dpi, a medium camera of 1280 x 960 dpi, and a high-end camera with a resolution of 1712 x 1368 dpi.

If digital photography interests you, start learning about them. Visit computer stores and camera shops to discuss your needs and budget. You can soon learn what's needed to do the job.

Technology has opened many new doors for home businesses over the past decade. The next decade will be even more exciting! And it can offer even greater profitability for your home business.

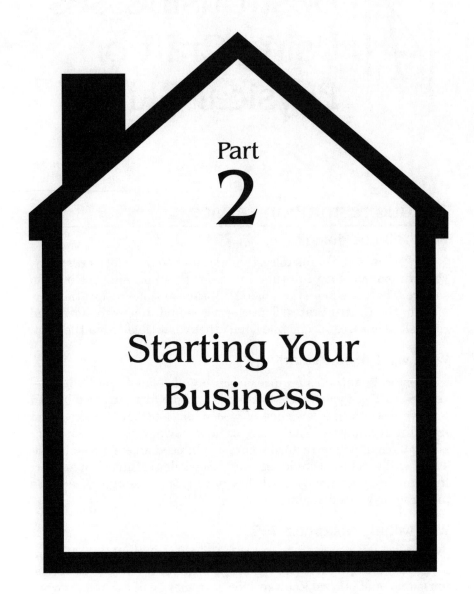

Part
2

Starting Your Business

4 Best Businesses Using Craft or Physical Skills

Antique restoration service

What will I be doing?

If you have the skills to restore antiques to their former beauty, you can make a good full-time income with an antique restoration service. There are more than 6,000 full-time antique restoration services in the United States. These services find, repair, restore, and refinish furniture, automobiles and other collectibles from the past.

What will I need to start?

Restoring antiques requires a variety of related and highly developed skills. If you decide to restore antique furniture you'll need to have a working knowledge of woods, old and new finishes, and finishing techniques. You'll also need woodworking and wood finishing tools. If you're restoring cars, you'll need an even wider variety of skills, tools, techniques, and knowledge. Many people start this business as a hobby until they have gained enough experience to attract paying customers.

Who will my customers be?

Your antique restoration knowledge and skills will be sold to individuals, antique dealers, resellers, estates, investors, galleries, museums, and others. Your specific customers will depend on what types of antiques you restore, your experience and the interest, and opportunities available in your area.

How much should I charge?

Antique restoration services typically earn $35 to $75 or more an hour. The wide variation of rates is based on the skills and the tools required for a particular job. Some restoration services can manage with a few hand tools while others will need an investment of many thousands of dollars to do a quality job. Most restoration services are priced on the value added. That is, a rough antique worth $100 that is restored into one now worth $1,000 should earn the restorer a fee based on the increased value rather than just the time and tools needed.

How much will I make?

Once established, an antique restoration service requires only about 10 to 20 percent of the owner's time to make sales calls and keep the books. However, overhead expenses can be higher in this home business than many others because of the investment in tools and equipment. Total overhead, including taxes, may be as high as 50 percent of earnings. Thus, a full-time antique restoration business that can sell $100,000 in services each year can keep $50,000 or more.

How can I get started?

To start a full-time antique restoration service, many people find, restore and resell pieces on their own. Others start this venture by working for someone else. A successful business requires advanced skills as well as a developed knowledge of both products and customers.

The SIC code for antique restoration services is 7641-12.

How can I use computers to increase profits?

Because of the size and fragile nature of antiques, most are restored locally. However, many antique restoration services learn about their trade and what restorers are doing in other parts of the world by using the Internet. They join newsgroups and trade associations. In addition, project management software helps them track the costs and income for specific restorations, helping them ensure that they make a reasonable profit.

Appliance installation and repair

What will I be doing?

Major appliances include washers, dryers, refrigerators, freezers, stoves, ovens, and many other products that we all rely on. Your business may simply install new appliances, picking them up at the appliance store, delivering them to the customer's homes, setting them up, and training the customer on use. Or you may also be able to offer a repair service for major appliances.

What will I need to start?

To install major appliances you'll need knowledge of how the appliances work, some tools, and a vehicle large enough to carry such appliances. To repair appliances, you'll need more knowledge and more tools. You'll also make more money. Consider starting an installation business until you've learned more about repairs.

Who will my customers be?

Customers for your appliance installation and/or repair service include both retail stores and consumers. One successful installer works through a discount appliance store, offering the store $5 per retail customer sent to him. The store doesn't install the appliances they sell so the service benefits everyone. Another successful appliance repair service offers annual contracts that include a semi-annual inspection of all major appliances and a discount on repairs.

How much should I charge?

Much of your work as an appliance installer or repair person will be priced on an hourly rate of $30 to $50. Once your business is tested, you'll be able to easily estimate the time needed to install a specific appliance or to make a common repair. You will then establish a flat fee for this service based on your hourly rate. Why? Because customers are sometimes reluctant to hire someone at $40 an hour but will pay $40 for a service (that *you* know will take you just an hour).

How much will I make?

Your home-based appliance installation and repair service can be very profitable if you can keep expenses down. Many do so by using tools and test equipment they already have as well as using an older car or pickup truck for service calls. (Of course, make sure you have your business name and telephone number on the vehicle for low-cost advertising.) An appliance installation and repair service will typically spend 25 to 35 percent of sales on overhead expenses. That means a full-time business that bills 30 hours a week at $40 an hour will have an income of $1,200 a week and be able to keep $600 to $900 after overhead expenses are paid.

How can I get started?

Your appliance installation and repair business may change focus a few times before you find the right combination of customers and services to make your home business profitable. Start by learning as much as you can about your trade. Also check regional telephone books for appliance parts houses and major appliance stores. Gather tools as needed. Select your vehicle if you don't already have one. (If you don't want to buy a truck just yet, find another home business that hauls for hire and get prices for hauling appliances!)

Contact local appliance stores who may hire you to do contract work for 75 to 90 percent of your standard hourly rate.

The SIC code for appliance stores is 5722-02.

How can I use computers to increase profits?

Appliance parts are readily available online. Using a model number you can search the parts bins of suppliers until you find what you need. There may even be a photograph to verify the part. Once an account is set up, you can order an in-stock part and typically have it shipped the same day. Also, the appliance factory may have its product manuals online for your review.

Automotive alarm installation

What will I be doing?

There's a growing need for services that select, install, test, repair, and service alarm systems for automobiles. Car owners in big cities and small towns alike are buying car alarms, but frequently don't know how to install them. That's where you can help.

What will I need to start?

To install car alarms you must first understand how automotive electrical systems work. You can pick up that knowledge in books available through larger bookstores as well as practicing on your own car(s). You may also be able to make copies of installation instructions for popular alarm systems.

You will need some tools and equipment as well: screwdrivers, pliers, wire cutters and strippers, electrical voltmeter, and a continuity tester. If you don't already have them, you can buy a basic set of tools and equipment for less than $100.

Who will my customers be?

Your customers will be those who have purchased or plan to purchase an auto alarm system. You can work through a retailer who will recommend you for installation or you can sell complete auto alarm packages yourself—installed and tested. Watching the newspaper's police report can tell you where potential customers are. Neighborhoods in which car theft is more prevalent are neighborhoods with prospective customers. A small advertisement in the automotive classified ads can help car buyers know about your services. You can also contract with auto alarm retailers to do their installation.

How much should I charge?

The rate for automotive alarm installation is typically $25 to $60 an hour with set rates based on typical installations. For example, you may charge a percentage of the value of the alarm system. One installer charges $50 for installing systems retailing under $200, and $75 for installing units up to $500 in value. He works by the hour for systems costing more than $500.

How much will I make?

An auto alarm installer can earn $500 or more in a day with overhead expenses of 20 to 30 percent. You can install the alarms in your garage, your driveway, at the car owner's home, or in a centrally located shop. The closer to home, the lower your overhead expenses will be. Unfortunately, a poor location may make attracting customers difficult. Remember that it's smarter to increase expenses if they proportionately increase income.

How can I get started?

Start by studying your competitors and how they work. If you have none, the market may be wide open. Then develop your knowledge and skills for installing auto alarms. Understand automotive electricity and how alarm systems work. Gather your tools. Get some experience by working for your friends or as an employee of a car alarm installation service. One successful installer with four years of experience started his business by taking on jobs his employer didn't want: installing alarms in big-rig trucks. He started a weekend business that soon became full-time.

The SIC code for automotive alarm installation services is 5531-07.

How can I use computers to increase profits?

Knowledge is power. There are hundreds of resources for automotive service businesses online. You can find out more about specific alarm systems, about the automobiles in which they are installed, and how to tackle problem installations. You can even look in on your local competitors to see how they price and warranty their services. You can also set up your own Web site to help potential customers select your services.

Auto detail service

What will I be doing?

An auto detail service professionally cleans, washes, waxes, and maintains the interior and exterior surfaces of cars, trucks, RVs, and other vehicles. There are more than 12,000 full-time auto detail services in the United States with thousands of them operating from homes and garages. This is a business you'll either love or hate. If you enjoy cars and enjoy making them look their best, you'll love this job. Otherwise, they couldn't pay you enough to do it. It's hard work.

What will I need to start?

To start an auto detailing service, all you really need is some time. You can begin by offering to wash and clean cars at a local car lot for an hourly rate or priced per car—on-the-job self-training. If you already have experience waxing and cleaning cars, you can apply this knowledge to your new business. If you know something about automotive paints and touchup, all the better.

Equipment is minimal. You can buy a power buffer later. For now, purchase quality wash, wax, and interior cleaning products. Use a washing bucket to hold everything. You'll soon learn which products work best for you at the least cost. Once learned, you can buy your products at wholesale or quantity prices.

Who will my customers be?

Your customers will include new car owners, classic car owners, new and used car dealers, trailer and motor home owners and dealers, boat owners and dealers, and just about anyone who owns a vehicle and cares about its appearance. You can specialize or work with a variety of vehicles.

How can you find customers? Place a small ad in the automotive section of a local newspaper. Prepare a flyer about your services and distribute it in parking lots, to car dealers, and post it on bulletin boards.

How much should I charge?

The hourly rate for an automotive detailer depends somewhat on your level of skills as well as on the value of the vehicle you're detailing. Cleaning clunker cars on a budget car lot won't earn you much—maybe $20 to $25 an hour if you work efficiently. However, detailing and touching up valuable new or classic cars can get you $35 to $50 an hour. As with other home-based businesses, use your hourly rate to calculate the price of a typical job. For example, a detailing that requires 45 minutes at $30 an hour should be priced at about $22.50.

How much will I make?

Once established, you'll only spend about 10 to 20 percent of your time marketing your business. The rest of the time will be spent detailing cars. Because you work out of your home, garage, or your own vehicle, your expenses are minimal. Detailing materials may cost $3 to $5 an hour. Overhead including taxes may take about 20 to 30 percent of every dollar you get. The other dollars are yours.

How can I get started?

First, learn your trade. Work as a detailer for a car lot or practice on your own and friends' cars. Read up on the subject. Have your car detailed by a service and watch how they do it. Also watch what products they use and how long it takes to use them.

Here's an idea for promoting your detailing service. One new detailer used a family car that had seen better years to show what can be done. She stretched masking tape through the middle of the car from front bumper to back, then completely detailed one half of the car. She did the same inside the car. Once done, she made a sign for the window telling about her auto detailing service. People could immediately see the results of her work and she developed many new customers by simply driving around.

The SIC code for an auto detail service is 7542-03.

How can I use computers to increase profits?

Amazingly, even auto detailers can use the Internet to enhance their profitability. Maguiers, Simoniz, and other car care product manufacturers have Web sites that offer product and application information. In addition, you can learn about local and regional car shows and plan to exhibit or to offer pre-show detailing services. Of course, you can also use computer software to make bookkeeping easier and give you more time to shine.

Beekeeper

What will I be doing?

Beekeepers raise and manage bees for honey and pollination services. Honey production is obvious, but what is a pollination service? Many agricultural crops, such as fruits, require pollination. This service is done by bees. During the appropriate time of the year the orchard owners call you to have beehives placed near trees. The bees do the rest.

"Wait a minute," you say. "What if I live in the city?" Can do. You can manage a small hive from a large lot or you can keep hives on a nearby farm.

What will I need to start?

You'll need bees. Besides that, you'll need a home for them— hives. You'll also need bee-handling equipment and a way of transporting the bees to farmers' fields. You'll also need some knowledge of bees and some experience handling them.

Where can you get these supplies and knowledge? Start by checking regional telephone books under "Beekeepers' Supplies" and related headings. They can help you get books and training on beekeeping as well as offer ideas on making your business work.

Who will my customers be?

Customers for your beekeeping service include retail and wholesale honey sellers as well as orchard owners and other agricultural enterprises. You can find them through local beekeeper supply houses, the Department of Agriculture extension offices, and the phone book.

How much should I charge?

Your fees as a beekeeper will vary depending on the products you sell and the services you provide. Most beekeepers sell honey by the pound and charge by the day or week for pollination services. Your hourly rate will range from $25 to $50. You will charge by the pound depending on the honey's floral source (clover, etc.), geographical source, and the difficulty in collecting it. Retail honey prices can range from $2 to $4 a pound or about $15 to $25 a gallon. The smaller the package, the higher the per-pound price. Your price in the city may be double that of your price in the country because of supply and demand.

How much will I make?

You will be able to charge for your time in working the hives for honey and for picking up and delivering hives to pollination sites. Most beekeepers don't make more than about $20,000 a year with this enterprise, and some much less. Instead, they use bees to supplement income from other sources. The exception is a full honey operation that includes packaging and marketing honey for wholesale and retail accounts. This venture can bring a net income of $40,000 a year or more once it is established.

How can I get started?

To start your beekeeping business, first learn as much as you can about bees. Find books, take courses, and tap into other resources for expanding your knowledge. Then, if you can, start small with a hive or two, learning how to manage bees. Simultaneously, begin looking for ways to sell your services. Talk with retailers about selling your honey. Speak with local farmers and orchard owners about pollination. Visit noncompeting bee handlers to learn what you can.

The SIC code for beekeepers is 4812-06.

How can I use computers to increase profits?

Beekeepers use computers to keep track of hive locations, weather conditions, agriculture alerts, and to keep in touch with other beekeepers. In fact, experienced beekeepers in other parts of the country can become your mentors to help you through the learning and selling processes. And you can "talk" with them daily via e-mail. In addition, some keepers sell honey products using Web sites, shipping around the world. (Be sure you know interstate and international agriculture law first.)

Bicycle repair service

What will I be doing?

Once a major mode of transportation, bicycles are still popular as recreation vehicles. They once were tools; now they're toys.

Fortunately, toys get attention when they're broken. A bicycle repair service maintains, repairs, restores, and recycles cycles. If you enjoy bicycle riding and happen to be handy with tools and repairs, consider starting your own bicycle repair service from your home or garage.

What will I need to start?

To fix bicycles, you must understand how they work. Though children's bikes are basic machines, those that adults ride are more sophisticated—and require more knowledge to repair.

One successful bicycle repair service began by purchasing children's bikes in any condition. He paid $10 if he could roll them away and $5 if he had to carry them. He then dismantled them, replaced parts as needed from other bikes, painted them and resold them at a profit. Some of the profit went toward attending factory schools for major bicycle brands. Within a few years, his weekend service had become a full-time bike shop specializing in racing bikes.

Who will my customers be?

Kids don't buy kids' bikes; parents and grandparents do. Adults also buy collector bikes, mountain bikes, racing bikes, and exercise bikes. So your customers will be adults buying for kids or the kid in themselves. Appeal to both the logic and the emotion of your customers and your business will succeed.

Most bicycle repair services promote themselves with small service ads in local newspapers, on area bulletin boards, in bike shops, and through referrals.

How much should I charge?

Although a bicycle repair service sets prices using an hourly rate, the price of most services is quoted to the customer based on the type of job or the value of the results. For example, a shop with a $30-an-hour rate may require 40 minutes to tune up a mountain bike. The price for this service isn't quoted as $30 an hour but as $20—or $19.95.

Base your pricing on your shop rate, the amount of time required for the typical job, and on the prices of your competitors. Keep your prices lower than those of your competitors—until you have too much business. Then raise them until you have just the right amount of business to keep you happy.

How much will I make?

No one has ever become rich repairing bicycles. However, many people have started small garage ventures that grew into lucrative bicycle businesses. So can you. Initially, you'll spend up to half of your time promoting your business, but should soon see that cut down to 25 percent of your time or less. Overhead expenses will depend on what type of business you're building, where you're located, and how much time you're devoting to it. Figure on keeping

50 to 75 percent of every dollar that comes in the door and you should be accurate.

So 40 hours a week means 30 billable hours a week. Multiply that by $25 an hour and you have a gross income of $600 a week. You'll probably be able to keep $400 to $500 after expenses.

How can I get started?

To start a bicycle repair business, learn as much as you can about bikes and how to repair them. Read bicycle magazines as well as additional resources such as books and associations that can help you build your business.

The SIC code for bicycle repair services is 7699-74.

How can I use computers to increase profits?

Bicycles have been around for more than a century, but computers are relatively new. Even so, computers can help your bicycle repair business in many ways. First, you can keep your business records using computer software. Second, you can share information with other repair shops using newsgroups and e-mail. Third, you can communicate with manufacturers via their Web sites. Fourth, you can set up your own Web site to build business, especially if you have a specialty that will draw regional or national customers.

Cabinetmaking service

What will I be doing?

There are over 18,000 professional cabinetmaking services in the United States, with many of them operating as home-based businesses. A cabinetmaking service designs and builds cabinets for new and re-modeled residences and businesses. Some cabinetmakers work directly with the owner while others prefer to work through contractors.

What will I need to start?

Making cabinets is a craft. Once you've learned the craft, you can offer your skills to others. So the first step to starting a cabinetmaking service is to build your skills. Learn cabinet construction, joinery, and production methods.

Second, start gathering your tools. To build cabinets you'll need both hand and power tools: saws, fastening equipment, finishing tools. Books on cabinetry will offer you advanced techniques as well as help in selecting the right tools.

Who will my customers be?

Customers for your cabinetmaking business include contractors, business owners and homeowners. Many cabinetmakers start by bidding on cabinets for a local residential contractor. A friendly contractor can not only help you get started but also serve as a professional reference to other customers.

You can develop new customers by advertising in local publications, especially those read by contractors and homeowners. Ads should stress the quality of your workmanship at affordable prices. Focus your advertising budget on professional service ads in newspapers and telephone books.

How much should I charge?

Your hourly rate as a cabinetmaker will range from $40 to $80. Of course, you typically won't tell your customers that rate. Instead, you will bid on jobs based on the time and materials spent on the project. Most professional cabinetmakers soon develop a multiplier, or per-unit price. For example, one cabinetmaker marks up the cost of materials 300 percent, pricing cabinets that require $1,000 in materials at $3,000. Others price by the linear foot of cabinets. Refer to my book, *The Woodworker's Guide to Pricing Your Work* (Betterway Books; available at *www.MulliganPress.com*) for more specific information on pricing wood products.

How much will I make?

Once your cabinetmaking service is established, you'll be able to get your shop rate for 70 to 80 percent of your time. That is, you can bill for 35 to 40 hours of a 50-hour week. Overhead expenses will take 25 to 50 percent of your net sales.

How can I get started?

Your cabinetmaking service will pay you for efficiency. That's what appeals to most men and women who get into this business. If you can make more cabinets in less time without reducing quality, you can make more money. So the key to success in this business is efficiency. That means buying equipment that helps you make more cabinets with the smallest investment. It also means learning techniques that make you a more efficient worker.

You will also profit from smart selling. Learn through experience who buys, how much they will pay, and how to keep them happy. You can start your cabinetmaking business in your spare time and build it to a full-time venture, learning as you earn.

The SIC code for cabinetmaking services is 1751-03.

How can I use computers to increase profits?

Cabinetmakers often have to develop cabinet designs using drafting equipment. The computer makes this easier through programs called Computer Aided Design, or CAD software. Some are specially made for cabinetry and finish carpentry. In addition to designing, many programs can also give you a three-dimensional representation of the cabinetry that will help you sell the finished product to your customer before the first boards are cut.

Carpentry service

What will I be doing?

You can turn your skills as a carpenter into a lucrative business that offers you an income greater than working for someone else. A carpenter designs and builds with lumber. Carpenters work in both remodeling and new construction. They use lumber to help build homes, storage buildings, business buildings, and other structures. They typically work as subcontractors to general building contractors.

What will I need to start?

Why would anyone hire a carpentry service to build something? Because the carpenter can build faster, more efficiently, and better than the person who does the hiring. So what you'll need to start your carpentry service is skill, efficiency, and knowledge of construction with lumber. You can get this advanced skill by attending a trade school or through on-the-job training working for someone else.

You'll also need some tools. The typical residential carpentry service has a pickup truck and/or utility trailer for transporting tools: power saws, fastening equipment, measuring tools, and materials. Many carpenters rely on air compressors to power nail guns and other fastening equipment. Some carpenters will also need heavy equipment for moving materials or even large ladders for reaching some jobs.

Who will my customers be?

Your customers will be general building contractors, other subcontractors, homeowners, business owners, and government contractors. Most carpentry services specialize in working with one or two types of customers because good reputations get around and bring them more business. For example, one carpentry service specializes in working with general contractors in the restaurant remodeling business. Focusing your business also makes it easier to find and keep customers.

How much should I charge?

The rate for carpentry services is typically $30 to $60 an hour depending on your market, competition, and skills. However, most services quote based on the typical job. They may price framing a new residence by the square footage or they may calculate a job using a day rate. Some rely on the general contractor to set the rate, accepting or rejecting it based on whether the carpentry service owner calculates that it will be profitable or not.

How much will I make?

Most services spend only 10 to 20 percent of available time marketing. This may be more in the beginning, but will diminish once established. Overhead expenses vary between 20 and 40 percent depending on a variety of factors. A one-person carpentry service in an area with mild climates and lots of new construction can earn the owner $60,000 to $90,000 a year.

How can I get started?

First, learn your trade. Develop your skills and reputation as an efficient carpenter by working hard and well for others. Learn the local building codes, develop friendships with contractors and others in the trade, take classes on construction and business.

Some carpentry services start out on weekends working with homeowners and business owners. They then build the business as dictated by local building opportunities and their reputation. Once ready to go full-time, they notify friends and professional contacts asking for business. Many advertise in local service directories.

The SIC code for carpentry services is 1751-02.

How can I use computers to increase profits?

Carpenters are using computers and computer technology for dozens of tasks, giving them more time to do their job. Software can help design decks and outdoor structures and CD-ROMs offer visual instructions on how to tackle new projects. Local building material suppliers can take orders and even confirm stock and schedule delivery over the Internet. In addition, project management software can help carpenters track numerous jobs and tasks more efficiently.

Carpet-cleaning service

What will I be doing?

There are more than 32,000 carpet-cleaning services in the United States, many operating as home-based businesses. A carpet-cleaning service, as you might expect, cleans carpets and rugs using special equipment. Typically, a home-based business will use the home as an office, but work from a vehicle parked at the customer's location.

What will I need to start?

You can start your carpet-cleaning service with just business cards or fliers passed to neighbors. Then, as you get a job, you rent a carpet-cleaning machine and buy the needed shampoo. As your business grows you can find used and new professional carpet-cleaning equipment at wholesale janitorial suppliers listed in metropolitan telephone books. These services can also suggest cleaning supplies.

Who will my customers be?

Customers for your carpet-cleaning service include homeowners, companies, and office buildings. Most carpet-cleaning services specialize in a specific market, focusing marketing on homeowners or apartment dwellers, office complexes, retail stores, shopping malls, or government offices. If your business is located in a large city and you have many competitors, you will specialize more than if your business serves a town of 10,000.

You can reach your customers through mailing lists, fliers, small service ads in newspapers, and ads in the yellow pages of area phone books.

How much should I charge?

You will calculate the prices of your services using an hourly rate, typically $25 to $50. However, you will quote the customer prices based on the size of the carpet cleaned and the need for cleaning. That is, you may charge 15 to 25 cents a square foot with the lower price for light cleaning and the higher price for carpets needing more work to clean.

Many carpet-cleaning services make pricing easier for the customer by quoting by the room. A 10 x 12-foot room of 120 square feet will range from $24 to $36, at 20 to 35 cents a square foot. So, the room rate can be quoted at $24.95 to $34.95 and require about a half-hour to clean. Most per-room rates require a minimum number of rooms, typically three, to reduce the time lost to setting up and taking down equipment at a site. In addition, some carpet-cleaning services add a specific price per room for moving furniture to clean the carpet.

How much will I make?

Initially, you'll spend up to half of your time marketing your business. But you will soon reduce that to 15 to 25 percent of your time through repeat and referral business. Overhead expenses will range from 20 to 40 percent of every dollar you take in, depending on the value of your equipment and how much you spend on marketing your services. A home-based carpet-cleaning business can earn $15 to $25 net per hour dedicated to the business.

How can I get started?

You can learn the skills required for efficiently cleaning carpets by working for a carpet cleaner or janitorial service. Doing so, you will also learn what equipment and supplies to use. If you maintain a good relationship with your employer, he or she may even help you establish your noncompeting business and even give or sell you accounts.

Contact the Carpet and Rug Cleaning Institute (706-278-3176). Franchises in this field include Rug Doctor (800-678-7844), Von Schrader Co. (800-626-6916) and Chem-Dry Carpet Cleaning (800-841-6583).

The SIC code for carpet-cleaning services is 7217-04.

How can I use computers to increase profits?

Carpet cleaning franchises and equipment manufacturers have found the Internet. So should you. For example, the Rug Doctor franchise is at *www.rugdoctor.com*. Von Schrader Co. is at *www.vonschrader.com*. Chem-Dry Carpet Cleaning is at *www.chemdry.com*. You can be on the Internet, too. Some franchisors offer links on their Web site to local franchisees.

Chimney sweep

What will I be doing?

There are more than 4,700 full-time chimney sweep services in the United States. The chimney sweep business is busiest in the fall and winter, and less busy in the spring and summer. So this is a good opportunity for those who work jobs or have other home businesses that are busier in the spring and summer. The income is good because it is a job that many people can't or don't want to do for themselves.

A chimney sweep service cleans residential and commercial chimneys and flues of soot and other by-products of fuel-burning heat systems. The job of cleaning chimneys, if done right, isn't as dirty as imagined. However, it typically requires that you climb up on roofs to operate the cleaning equipment.

What will I need to start?

Chimney cleaning isn't rocket science. However, it does require a working knowledge of how to efficiently clean chimneys without dirtying your customer's home or office. If you don't have experience in this task, find books that explain the process and the needed tools. You can also learn about chimney sweeps by hiring one. If your home doesn't have a chimney or you live in an apartment, hire one for a friend who has a chimney and watch the sweep at work.

Who will my customers be?

Your customers will be homeowners, business owners, apartment building owners, and commercial building owners. You may decide to specialize in one type or another, or you may even expand your business to include selling heating system components.

Go after your customers through advertising and fliers. Call on local fireplace shops and heating system suppliers.

How much should I charge?

The hourly rate for a chimney sweep service, including labor and overhead costs, is typically $25 to $50. However, most sweeps price their services by the job. They may charge by the number of flues, their length and size, the time since last cleaned, and other factors. If your business is just starting out, consider pricing your service lower than that of your competitors to develop business. Once you're established and have a reputation for good work and service, you can increase your prices accordingly.

How much will I make?

Initially, up to one-third of your time will be spent marketing your business. As your sweep business grows, more of your time will be billable. If your time is limited, a spouse or friend can help you by handling the marketing and scheduling while you do the jobs.

About 60 to 80 percent of everything you make will be yours to keep—at least for a few minutes. The 20 to 40 percent of expenses will cover tools, transportation, home office expenses, taxes, and other necessities of business. So a full-time chimney service that can keep busy an average of 30 hours a week can earn the owner a salary of $25,000 to $50,000 a year.

How can I get started?

To start your chimney sweep business, first learn your trade either by reading and watching or, better, by working for a chimney sweep service. Working for others can help you determine whether this is the right business for you while it helps you develop efficient skills that can make you more money.

The SIC code for chimney sweep services is 7349-16.

How can I use computers to increase profits?

Chimney sweeps use computers to keep customer records, track income and expenses, correspond with franchisors, spy on competitors, and find new customers. Computers are best for managing customer information and preparing mailings to remind customers when it's time to schedule another cleaning. Remembering your customers will help them remember you.

Construction cleanup service

What will I be doing?

If you want to be paid to exercise, consider starting your own construction cleanup service. Residential and commercial buildings that have just undergone construction are a mess. Carpenters, electricians, plumbers, and other subcontractors build quickly and efficiently, throwing waste aside for someone else to clean up. You can offer to clean up the site for an hourly rate, a flat fee based on the size of the building, or for a reduced rate if you can recycle waste.

Specifically, construction cleanup services pick up trim and waste from excavation, drywall, electrical, plumbing, roofing, and other contractors. They do this after hours, evenings and on weekends when workers aren't on-site, putting in as many as 45 hours a week.

What will I need to start?

There are few skills required to clean up a construction site. However, the owners and contractors are trusting you to pick up only waste and not good materials. Develop this trust into a relationship of honesty and your business will grow.

You will need safety equipment to ensure that you don't step on nails or are injured by other materials. You will probably need to be licensed and bonded, as are other subcontractors. You may need a truck to haul away materials, though some services keep a large dumpster at the site where materials can be placed during cleanup.

Who will my customers be?

Your customers for a construction cleanup service are building contractors and subcontractors. You may work directly with a general contractor responsible for a group or subdivision of homes or a large commercial building. Or you may be hired by an electrical or plumbing contractor to clean up after their crews and recycle what you can. Check your area telephone books for contractors.

One enterprising construction cleanup service also rented outdoor toilets to construction sites. Not only did it add to income, it also gave the service a prominent place to advertise!

How much should I charge?

Construction cleanup doesn't require extensive skills or training. The work is physically demanding and does require that you learn to work efficiently. The hourly rate for a construction cleanup service is $20 to $45. However, the service is usually priced by the size of the job, measured in square feet, and the difficulty. For example, you may be hired to clean up a group of 12 new homes of 2,000 square feet each for a month. If you calculate that the total time will be about 120 hours and you charge $25 an hour, your fee will be $3,000. Divide that amount by the square footage and you come up with 12.5 cents per square foot. If you find that your time estimate was accurate, you can bid future jobs at 10 cents per square foot for easy jobs and 15 cents per square foot for difficult jobs, with the average rate at 12.5 cents per square foot.

How much will I make?

Once you've established your business and developed some experience, most of your time will be spent working rather than selling your services. In fact, you may ask someone in your family to take calls, quote jobs, and schedule your time. If so, you can be more productive and more profitable. Remember to deduct for overhead, including a pickup truck or a car and utility trailer as needed. Calculating overhead at 20 percent income and estimating about 1,600 billable hours each year at $25 an hour, your annual net income can be about $32,000.

How can I get started?

Do you know any contractors? If so, talk with them about your service. Offer to do one job for free if they will show you what to do and give you a reference when done. If you don't know any contractors, call a few and offer your services. After you've done a couple of jobs, produce a flyer listing your services, references, and prices, then circulate it to job sites and mail it to contractors.

Don't forget to check with state and local construction licensing offices as your area may require licensing, bonding, certification, or other regulations for your service. Many construction cleanup services start by working weekends, then building the business into a full-time venture as soon as possible.

How can I use computers to increase profits?

How can construction cleanup services use computers to make more money? They can tap into city hall. Many cities and counties post information about new building permits on their Internet Web site. These building permits tell you about potential customers for your service. If your local government doesn't offer this service, try to find newsletters that publish this information. They often have an online version of their newsletter—for a fee. But this information is valuable to you.

Dog breeder

What will I be doing?

If you enjoy dogs, raising and selling them may be the perfect home business for you. It can be both demanding and rewarding. Dog breeders raise dogs for specific functions, such as for show or for pets. A few breeders do both, selecting breeding stock and pups based on the breed standards and the temperament of the animals.

What will I need to start?

To successfully breed dogs you must know a lot about them. You must also love them. However, many breeders find that building a business around dogs can sometimes strain the relationships and make them less fun. So knowing your own limits can help you learn whether this is the best home business for you.

You must develop an extensive knowledge of your product: dogs. Join local and national kennel clubs, begin building your reference library, talk with other breeders, start gathering equipment and tools and find out who your customers will be. The space required, number, size and type of kennel units, breeding equipment, and other factors depend on what type of dog you're breeding, typical size, whether you are breeding show or family dogs and how much of their health needs (shots, etc.) you manage yourself. The AKC and breed associations can help you with specific requirements.

Who will my customers be?

You will have many types of customers from which to choose, depending on the breed and type of dog you are raising. In fact, if you are showing your breed, one of your customers will be you. Other customers include individuals who want to have a dog for show or companionship, associations that train dogs for the handicapped, and pet stores who will sell dogs directly to the public.

How much should I charge?

Because breeding dogs is a labor of love for so many people, competition is high and profit hard to get. If your investment of time requires that you sell a dog for $750, how can you compete with a hobbyist offering a similar animal for $250? You can't. Instead, you must find breeds that appeal to those who know the difference in quality of animals and who are willing to pay for that difference.

In general, dog breeders price dogs by the quality and use of the animal. A show-quality dog may get a price of $800 to $1,000, while a family pet from the same litter may go for under $500. The investment is the same, but the use is different.

How much will I make?

Dog breeders may take years to develop skills in selection and reputation as a quality breeder before they make much money. Once established, a breeder can sell $25,000 to $75,000 in dogs a year, keeping about half the money and spending the rest on overhead expenses.

How can I get started?

The dog business, like every other, is one of supply and demand. If there is a greater supply than demand for a specific breed, prices go down, and vice versa. So look to breeds that aren't in great supply locally, but are coming into demand. In fact, breeders work hard to develop demand by promoting their breed. So can you.

Of course, read magazines like *Dog Fancy* and join organizations like the American Kennel Club (AKC) for additional resources.

The SIC code for dog breeders is 0752-07.

How can I use computers to increase profits?

Dog breeders are organized: AKC, special breed organizations, and show promoters. That means they're on the Internet. Check the literature from groups of which you're a member and you'll probably see a URL or Web address printed on it. In addition, there are dozens of newsgroups specifically for various dog breeds. Joining one (it's free) opens you up to a new world of people with common interests and a computer.

Errand/delivery service

What will I be doing?

It seems like so many home businesses require special training, a degree, or a rich uncle. Not so in the delivery business. In fact, few skills are needed and your greatest assets are a hard-working attitude—and a reliable vehicle.

What does an errand or delivery service do? It travels locally for others. It's a taxi service for things rather than for people. What kind of things? Pizza, packages, prescriptions, pets, plants, and more. That's up to you and your customers.

What will I need to start?

Your errand/delivery service will require a vehicle—but it doesn't have to be a truck or even a car. Depending on where you live and what you deliver, a bicycle or motorcycle may be a fine vehicle for the job. A good area map and knowledge of the roads and neighborhoods of your city are also important.

Who will my customers be?

There are so many potential customers for your errand or delivery service that it's difficult to know where to start. Here are a few prospective customers: doctors' offices (delivering records or test bottles), shut-ins (groceries, medicines, mail), restaurants (delivering take-out food), businesses (delivering small packages or important records to customers), trucking services (picking up and delivering small packages), etc.

How much should I charge?

You can charge for your services by the mile or by the job, but your pricing will be based on a combination of time and expenses. For example, you may decide to charge $20 an hour for your time and 50 cents a mile for your car. Or you may charge $25 an hour for you and your bike. You may have a higher rate for emergency ("I need it *now*") errands and a lower one for less critical runs that can be combined with other runs.

How much will I make?

Income for your errand or delivery service will depend primarily on your ability to get customers. You may decide to contract with one or two local restaurants for the evening hours while leaving your afternoon hours open for trips to the grocery store or pharmacy. Once you've learned how to promote your business, your income will grow.

Income for your full-time business will range from $15,000 to $30,000 a year with potential for more if you hire additional people. Expenses will include fuel and insurance for your vehicle, advertising, and a telephone. Consider a cellular telephone that you can answer wherever you are.

How can I get started?

If you're considering starting a home-based errand or delivery service (or both), start looking around for competitors. Watch local restaurant ads for any reference to delivery. (Idea: if one restaurant offers food delivery, go to a competing restaurant and offer to do the same for them.)

Be sure to talk with your insurance agent about coverage and costs. Depending on what you're doing, you may need to get commercial insurance. You may even need a special permit in your city. Keep your eyes open for traffic—and opportunities!

The SIC code for delivery services is 4212-05.

How can I use computers to increase profits?

Lost? Global Positioning Satellites, or GPS, can tell you where you are and, more importantly, how to get where you want to be. As you've probably guessed, GPS units use computer chips to track and display. You can buy a GPS for a few hundred dollars (some luxury cars include them), or you can use a notebook computer and cellular phone in your car or truck to log on to the Internet and access one of the mapping services such as *www.randmcnally.com*.

Floral service

What will I be doing?

There are more than 50,000 floral services in the United States. How can you operate a home business in what is traditionally a retail storefront enterprise? You can offer supporting services.

For example, your home-based floral business may arrange or deliver flowers for florist shops. Or you may grow them at your home, selling them wholesale to the shops or to floral wholesalers. Or you may produce products sold through florist shops such as vases, dry-flower arrangements, or trim products.

What will I need to start?

To successfully start a floral service you'll need to know your products, whatever they may be. You may specialize in potted geraniums or in holiday arrangements. Whatever your specialty, you must know much more about it than your customers. The more you know, the more you will profit.

You will also need skills, resources, and equipment. If you're a flower arranger, you'll need related skills, flowers to arrange and a work area. If you offer delivery services, you'll need to have a vehicle, a safe driving record, knowledge of the city, and be available for quick deliveries.

Who will my customers be?

Customers for your floral service will include individuals (funerals, weddings) businesses, churches, and other groups. Some home-based floral services specialize in a type of product or customer. One successful service provided floral arrangements for local churches on a contract basis. Each week featured a new arrangement. Because the arrangements at all customer churches were the same, she was able to buy in quantity at the nearby floral wholesale market. She bought on Saturday morning, arranged all day Saturday and delivered early Sunday morning.

Defining the customers of your floral service will depend on what you sell.

How much should I charge?

Floral services typically establish an hourly rate of $25 to $60, but price by the arrangement. Others use multipliers such as four-times-wholesale. Others, especially floral services that are starting out, price slightly lower than competitors in order to develop business.

For more information on pricing floral services, read my book, *Upstart Guide to Owning and Managing a Florist Service* (Upstart Publishing) available at *www.MulliganPress.com*.

How much will I make?

Your florist service will require 10 to 30 percent of your time for marketing, depending on what you provide and to whom you sell. That means 70 to 90 percent of the time you devote to your business is billable. You'll probably need more marketing time as you begin, but may eventually spend less as your reputation grows.

Overhead costs vary greatly depending on the type of product or service your provide. If you're producing arrangements on your kitchen table, overhead will probably be low. Including taxes, it may be as low as 20 percent. However, if you need a shop or delivery equipment, overhead may take 40 to 50 percent of every dollar you make. Even so, a full-time home-based floral service can earn $30,000 or more each year. Some do even better.

How can I get started?

To start your business, first learn your trade. If you are selling your arrangement skills, attend a floral trade school or read up on these skills and get a job in the industry. Keep an eye out for opportunities in the industry where you would like to serve others—and make money from home.

The SIC code for floral services is 5992-01.

How can I use computers to increase profits?

Computers have virtually revolutionized the florist industry. It started well before 1-800-FLOWERS as florists and trade associations across the country linked themselves together in computer networks, sharing information. Today there are numerous national floral delivery services on the Internet. In addition, florists are using the Internet to order as well as to sell. Of course, florists also use computers for accounting, e-mail, and learning more about their trade and how to increase profits.

Food delivery service

What will I be doing?

We live in a take-out society. Every year, the number of meals eaten away from home increases—as does the number of restaurant meals eaten at home. This is where a food-delivery service can make money. A food-delivery service, obviously, delivers prepared foods to customers. Not as obvious is the related services a food-delivery business can offer: grocery delivery, video delivery, even package delivery.

What will I need to start?

To deliver food to homes you'll not only need a vehicle, you'll need one that can carry food safely and efficiently. Because of fuel fumes, the food should not be placed in the trunk, but should ride with the driver. You may need to replace a seat with an insulated box or install one in a van.

You may also need to obtain a food handler's license or certificate, and maybe a commercial vehicle license, depending on your state and county requirements. Who would tell if you're using a car without proper licensing? Your competition!

You will also need a cellular telephone so customers can contact you while you're on the road.

Who will my customers be?

Who will hire you to deliver food and other perishables? In most cases, you'll be working for the restaurants who want to sell more take-out food. Your customers may also include caterers and even individuals.

One successful food-delivery service specialized in delivering fast-food products made and sold at a local shopping mall. The owner/driver picked up orders at the back door, placed them in insulated boxes and headed out. The restaurants knew that the service would be at the back door on the hour and half-hour between 4 and 9 p.m., seven days a week, and timed food preparation to match these times. Customers knew it, too, and called in orders asking for delivery.

In a smaller town with fewer restaurants, an enterprising delivery service took lunch orders for a factory, then placed the orders with area restaurants and timed delivery for noon. Another developed a pizza-and-a-movie order system that kept her busy full-time.

How much should I charge?

Your food-delivery service will establish an hourly rate of $20 to $40, but price in other ways. Some services charge the restaurant a percentage of the bill, typically about 20 percent, with a minimum delivery charge of $2 per delivery. Others charge by the mileage, comparable to the price established by local taxi companies. A few specialize in one or two restaurants, contracting by the hour. Tips are kept by the driver.

How much will I make?

"Hustle" is the name of this business. If you can safely and efficiently deliver food when people want it, you can make good money—

and even better tips. In fact, full-time food-delivery services can earn $20,000 to $30,000 profit a year. Make sure that you drive within the speed limits and obey other traffic laws; unsafe driving is not good for business or customer relations.

How can I get started?

Begin studying local opportunities. Find out if someone else is already offering such a service and, if so, how can you do it better or for a different customer. Also consider cooperating with another delivery service, defining territories that are efficient for both while combining your marketing efforts.

Also look at unique ways to promote your service with a catchy name (Dan's Mobile Diner) or symbol (a chef on a bicycle). The more people who see your delivery vehicle—clean and safely driven—the more they will think of you when they want restaurant food at home.

Once you've designed and tested your food-delivery service, produce a brochure or flyer and hand it out to restaurants that may hire your business. Also ask friends to call restaurants asking if they offer delivery service.

How can I use computers to increase profits?

This is a business that has taken off on the Internet during the past few years. Today, you can order prepared food or even groceries via the Internet and have them delivered to your home. Some services will even put the groceries away for you. But Internet grocery services are only in a few major cities right now (soon to change, I'm sure). Meantime, consider working with local grocers in your area to offer both prepared food and grocery delivery services to your customers.

Furniture upholstery service

What will I be doing?

This is the perfect home business for people who enjoy working with their hands. A furniture upholstery service, as you certainly guessed, upholsters or reupholsters furniture. Some purchase frames and add padding and materials to make a new piece of furniture while others renovate old upholstered furniture to look like new. Some do both.

What will I need to start?

Upholstering furniture is a skill that can be learned in a classroom, on the job, or it can be self-taught at home. It takes lots of practice to develop skills that can be sold, but it is a rewarding business in many ways, including financially.

Upholstering furniture requires tools, equipment and materials. It is an excellent home business because a garage can easily be converted into both a work area and a show room. The work area is typically a 4 x 4-foot worktable with the top 18 to 24 inches above the floor, depending on the type of furniture being upholstered. Materials are stored on rolls mounted on one wall or on the ceiling. Upholstery tools are kept on a stationary or portable workbench. An industrial sewing machine can be mounted on its own table.

Who will my customers be?

You can sell your furniture upholstery services to individuals, businesses, furniture stores, and small furniture manufacturers. Some shops try working with all of these customers until they find the best market for their services. Others have more experience with one or another customer group and initially serve them.

One successful furniture upholstery service began her business by purchasing used chairs with damaged upholstery but good frames for less than $25 each, reupholstering them, and selling them through classified ads for about half the price of new units. Not only did she build her business, but she also built her skills.

How much should I charge?

Upholsterers typically charge by the piece depending on the estimated time to upholster. The shop rate set by many upholsters is $30 to $70 an hour. Material costs are added on. For example, reupholstering a chair may take two hours at $35 an hour plus $30 in materials. The price is set at $100. Alternately, the upholsterer can have two grades of material, offering one at $100 and another at $125 per chair. The better grade of materials may not cost an extra $25, but the perceived value is higher so the price is too.

How much will I make?

Once your business is going and your tools are paid for, most of what you get in sales will be yours to keep—until the tax man takes his share! With a good reputation and some local advertising, a furniture upholstery shop can bill for 80 to 90 percent of the workday and spend 20 to 40 percent on overhead expenses. That means the owner can keep $40,000 to $60,000 once the business is established and running efficiently.

How can I get started?

You will be paid for both your skill and your efficiency in upholstering furniture. So, to build a profitable business you'll need to be both skillful and efficient. Start now learning the trade, expanding your skills, finding customers, gathering equipment, learning about materials, designing your shop, and outsmarting your competitors.

The SIC for a furniture upholstery service is 7641-09.

How can I use computers to increase profits?

Many furniture upholsters build a competitive edge by purchasing materials and supplies via the Internet. They can do so when it's convenient for them rather than for a salesperson. They can learn more about the material before buying. They can request immediate shipping if necessary. In addition, upholsterers use computers to network with other upholsterers and learn more about their trade.

Gardening service

What will I be doing?

If *your* garden grows well, consider offering your green thumb—and your knowledge—to others for money. A gardening service selects, plants, and maintains vegetable plants, flowers, and shrubs. There are many ways to turn your talents as a gardener into a profitable home-based business. You may design flower gardens for the front entrances of local businesses. You may offer answers to questions about eradicating garden pests. You may do soil analysis, give classes on better gardening, or even tend a garden for folks on vacation. Use your imagination.

What will I need to start?

To offer a professional gardening service you must know more than other people do about raising a successful vegetable or flower garden. What you will need to start, of course, is lots of experience with gardens. You'll also need some resources such as books on plants and their care. You may need some gardening tools. It will help if you've taken advanced courses on plant care, especially ones that offer certificates. The more you know, the more you will profit.

Who will my customers be?

Most individuals won't pay you very much for your gardening services. You can offer consumer classes, answer questions through a newspaper or magazine column, or answer questions for customers of a local garden shop. But most of your business will come from businesses. Companies who can profit from well-designed grounds, flower beds, and related plantings will be good customers. You may even participate in their care, depending on what type of gardening service you offer. A garden service sold the idea of planting and maintaining a large vegetable garden on one company's vacant property, then donating the food to local charities. Everyone benefited.

How much should I charge?

Gardening services use a rate of $20 to $40 an hour for pricing their work by the job or on long-term contract. A local newspaper may pay $20 (and offer lots of valuable publicity) for a weekly gardening column that takes you an hour or less to write. A garden shop may pay you $100 for a four-hour Saturday clinic on gardening. A business may pay you $1,200 a year for selecting and maintaining a flower bed in front of their office.

How much will I make?

A gardening service certainly isn't a get-rich-quick business. However, watching for opportunities to promote your business can pay off. A gardening service that specialized in designing colorful flowerbeds gave the owner a chance to write and illustrate a book that has earned more than $10,000 in royalties.

You can make $20,000 to $40,000 a year with a successful gardening service that is well-marketed to businesses and individuals in the area. Equally important, it can be a satisfying occupation that brings happiness to you as well as to others.

How can I get started?

Start today by looking for opportunities to sell your gardening services in your area. Look at the weekend section of local newspapers for ads, resources, ideas, and opportunities to find and help customers. Make a list of services you're qualified to offer to others, then list those who may best benefit from them. And watch your gardening service grow!

The SIC code for gardening services is 0782-06.

How can I use computers to increase profits?

Gardeners use computers to communicate with experts on the best selection, maintenance, and use of specific plants, shrubs, and trees. They use professional forums to discuss diseases. They order stock from regional nurseries. And they promote their services via the Internet.

Gift basket service

What will I be doing?

The gift basket business has nearly $1 billion in annual sales with more than 10,000 outlets. Some are in shopping malls, but a growing number are home-based businesses.

As the owner of a gift basket service, you may design, assemble, and deliver unique gifts on behalf of businesses and individuals. Most gift baskets have a theme or a focus: birthday, holiday, get well, beauty, etc. Not all are delivered in baskets. Some gifts are delivered in ornamental bags, large decorated tins, wooden boxes, and other containers that fit the theme.

What will I need to start?

There are thousands of gift basket services in the United States, so yours must be unique to survive, not to mention thrive. Have you ever bought or received a gift basket? If so, what did you like—or not like—about it? What are other gift basket services in your area offering? Knowing what you can do that is unique will help you start a successful gift basket service.

You can gather gifts and materials from a variety of sources. To keep costs down, you will want to buy everything at wholesale prices. Some services buy from floral supply houses while others find what they need at large wholesale craft outlets. A few order through national catalogs offered in trade publications such as *Gift Basket Review* (904-634-1902).

Who will my customers be?

Customers for your gift baskets include individuals, companies, agencies, associations, and groups, depending on what you decide to sell and what your competitors are offering. For example, you can specialize in award baskets for fraternal organizations, birthday baskets for customers of your business clients, or travel gift baskets for those who stay at your client's bed and breakfast inn. Be creative.

How much should I charge?

Though gift basket services establish a rate of $25 to $40 an hour, they typically charge by the basket based on materials and labor. Some use a markup of two or three times the price of the gifts while others set a price and build a basket that offers a reasonable profit. Most gift baskets range from $25 to $90 with some businesses paying more for special baskets for clients.

How much will I make?

Your gift basket service will be seasonal with lots of business around holidays and little in between—unless you learn how to market your services well. Good marketing will make a difference in your income. A holiday business can bring you an income of $10,000 a year or less with a well-marketed business offering the owner an income of $35,000 a year or more. Sell service!

Overhead expenses for your venture will range from 15 to 30 percent after you've paid for the gifts themselves. This percentage covers home office, telephone, advertising, and related business expenses.

How can I get started?

The best way to find customers for your gift basket service is to become a customer yourself. Start looking for other services in your area and interviewing them about their offerings. Check the telephone book for gift and basket wholesalers. Some services start by volunteering to make up gift baskets for a local organization in exchange for a letter of reference. The experience will be valuable to you.

The SIC code for gift basket services is 5947-13.

How can I use computers to increase profits?

Gift baskets ship easily. That means your customers don't have to be those who live nearby. You can sell to the world. Of course, you must make your products either unique or less expensive. For example, a gift basket service on the Oregon coast added small myrtlewood products available locally in his gift baskets sent worldwide. Consider using the Internet to sell your products.

Handyperson service

What will I be doing?

Some people love variety. They want a business that will challenge them every day. They enjoy being a jack- or jill-of-all-trades. And they love working with their hands.

To match these skills, many people need someone who is "handy" to do a variety of odd jobs: hauling, painting, fixing, building, stacking, or trimming. So the solution is to match those who need and those who are handy. That's actually the easy part.

What will I need to start?

To be handy is to be skilled and clever with your hands. To be a handyperson is to have a variety of skills and to not be afraid of learning new ones. The more you learn the more you earn. To start a handyperson service you will also need some tools. You'll need transportation such as a pickup truck. One enterprising handyperson took the back seat out of an old family sedan, removed the barrier between the seat and the trunk, and was able to haul everything from plywood and lumber to cans of paint in the space.

Gather together your tools—you may have everything you need right now. A handyperson who was asked to paint a shed purchased the equipment needed for the job and was able to use the equipment for dozens of later painting jobs.

You may also need a license or permit. Check with the state or local contractor licensing board to find out. If you must, remember that the licensing is intended to protect your customers. Make the best of it.

Who will my customers be?

As a handyperson, you will find that most of your customers will probably be homeowners. In fact, you may decide to specialize in helping homeowners in a specific part of your town. Or you may prefer cleaning and hauling jobs over painting and wallpapering. Another handyperson may decide to work for shop owners as they renovate an older downtown commercial area. And yet another might do cleanup work at a small industrial park, taking loads of scrap to the dump and used boxes to the recycler.

If your customers live in a geographic area, spend a few days taking your fliers door to door. Talk with potential customers and find out what types of jobs they need.

How much should I charge?

A handyperson can establish an hourly rate of $20 to $50, depending on skills and equipment. For example, a handyperson who tends lawns with little equipment requirements may be on the low side of the scale while one with a hauling truck and lots of skills and tools may be on the higher side.

With experience, you'll find that you're doing the same three or four types of jobs over and over. Thought it may sound boring, there is still variety. Better, it will help you become more efficient and make your estimates more accurate. You can then look at a job and quote an accurate price to the customer without revealing your hourly rate.

"Trimming up these bushes will cost just $15 if I can do it next week when I'm in the neighborhood." You calculated the job as needing a half-hour with an hourly rate of $30 an hour. The customer calculates that the same job would take him two hours and is willing to trade the 15 bucks for two extra hours on the golf course. Everybody wins.

How much will I make?

Initially, you will spend most of your time finding customers and jobs. Once established, about 25 percent of your time will be needed for marketing your services and quoting jobs. Your overhead expenses will depend on the cost of your equipment and the amount of advertising you must do to attract business. Overhead expenses, including taxes, will range from a low of 20 percent to as much as 50 percent of every dollar of income.

How can I get started?

First, decide whether you need licenses, permits, or bonding for your handyperson service. If so, get them—or at least know how to get them once you're ready to start your business.

Second, identify your knowledge and skills. Then think about who might be willing to trade money for these skills. Next, talk to a few of these people to make sure your thinking is accurate. Also ask them what they would be willing to pay for a specific job. Looking at the job, estimate the time needed and decide whether you can earn a fair fee for your time. If so, try to get the job.

How can I use computers to increase profits?

A handyperson typically can't find new customers on the Internet, but he or she can find materials and knowledge. For example, a handyperson asked to help restore an old stairway banister found parts in an online renovation catalog. He then posted a message to a newsgroup to which he subscribed describing the problem. Within hours he had numerous responses with solutions.

Home and business alarm service

What will I be doing?

A home and business alarm service gets paid for selecting, designing, installing, and maintaining alarms for individual and commercial accounts. This is not the same as a security service. An alarm service focuses on alarm equipment, leaving additional security methods and devices to others.

What will I need to start?

To establish a profitable alarm service you'll need a working knowledge of how electrical alarm systems work. This will require training in electronics and intrusion alerting systems. You can get this knowledge and experience on the job working for an alarm or security service, or you can get training through a local college or trade school.

You'll also need tools for installing and repairing alarm systems. You can purchase a complete set of electrical tools for less than $500, including testing meters. You may also need a commercial vehicle for your tools and equipment.

In addition, you will need a wholesale source of alarm equipment. You can find this resource in metropolitan telephone books, at electrical supply houses, and through ads in electrical industry magazines.

Who will my customers be?

Some alarm systems specialize in working with either homeowners or commercial businesses, but you may have to sell to both until your business grows. Much depends on the local market for alarm systems, what your competitors are and aren't doing, and your own skills and experience.

Most alarm systems services promote themselves through advertisements in the telephone book or local publications. Some promote the business by putting on free home security workshops or offering free security inspections of businesses. Others work under contract to security services.

How much should I charge?

Your rate for installing and maintaining alarm systems will be based on a $30 to $75 per hour rate. You will price your work on a markup, a flat installation fee, or on a monthly maintenance contract that is estimated based on your hourly rate. For example, you may sell a $500 alarm system for $1,000 installed, estimating that it will take you about 10 hours (at $50 an hour) to complete the typical installation. A maintenance contract that includes an estimated one-hour-a-month inspection and troubleshooting can be priced at your hourly rate.

How much will I make?

As your business is built, you'll be able to bill for 75 to 90 percent of your time. Excluding the cost of products you sell, your overhead will be 25 to 40 percent depending on the cost of operating your trade vehicle. So a successful home and business alarm service can earn the owner a gross income of $25,000 to $60,000 a year.

How can I get started?

There are too many fly-by-night businesses out there. To compete with them, make sure you have developed valuable knowledge and skills in your trade. Then find a way of letting others know they can trust you. Get certified. Join trade associations. Be helpful and friendly.

Begin gathering tools and equipment. Also find sources of quality alarm components. Get installation manuals from the wholesaler or factory that can help you do the job well in the least time.

Study your competitors and plan how you will promote your business. Come up with a business name that is both easy to remember and instills trust.

The SIC code for alarm services is 5063-24.

How can I use computers to increase profits?

Home alarm services often sell their services by helping prospects visualize the system. This takes some drawing skills—or some drawing software. Using a blocking graphic program like Microsoft Visio can help you easily lay out the system on paper to show how the system works. It can later guide you during installation. In addition, home alarm businesses typically use accounting software to manage income and expenses.

Housecleaning service

What will I be doing?

It's a busy world! Two-income families don't have time to clean house. With all the cleaning needing to be done in this country, it's no wonder there are 28,000 full-time housecleaning services in the United States!

There are many reasons why people need a housecleaning service. If you have the skills to efficiently clean houses—or are willing to learn them—you can set up a home-based housecleaning service for extra cash.

A housecleaning service cleans windows, vacuums carpets, washes floors and counters, dusts furniture and drapes, and does other general cleaning. These services typically do not "pick up" after clients or do laundry or dishes. Some cleaning services specialize in homes, others do apartments, and a few specialize in cleaning offices and other businesses.

What will I need to start?

You may have all the basic cleaning equipment you need in your home right now. You may also have supplies, but maybe not in economical quantities. If not, shop the discount warehouse stores or wholesale janitorial supply stores for them. The janitorial suppliers may even recommend supplies better for the task or offer techniques for using them more efficiently.

Make sure you have efficient cleaning skills. To earn the highest hourly rate you will need to develop skills that help you get the jobs done quickly and well. Books like *Clutter's Last Stand* (Betterway Books) are helpful to the entrepreneurial house cleaner.

Who will my customers be?

Customers for your housecleaning service are homeowners, apartment dwellers, and even businesses. For efficiency, you may prefer to specialize in homes within a limited geographic area to limit time between jobs. Your customers may also be homebuyers or renters referred to you by real estate agents in your area.

You can reach potential clients with a flyer taken door-to-door and to local real estate offices. As you give the flyer out, ask if there are any jobs you can bid on while you're there. You may get a job on the spot.

How much should I charge?

The typical hourly rate for a housecleaning services is $25 to $45 depending on your location and competition. The higher rate goes to experienced cleaners who have developed shortcuts and lots of referral business. Until then, establish your rate on the lower end of the scale.

As with other home-based businesses, you probably won't quote your hourly rate to the customer. Instead, you will give a single price for the job. However, you will set that price by multiplying the estimated time (based on your experience) times your hourly rate.

"I can vacuum the entire house, dust furniture and drapes, clean floors and counters, wash all windows inside and out and clean bathrooms and kitchens for just $95 per visit." You've calculated that you can do the jobs in three hours at $30 an hour and use about $5 in supplies. (The customer is thinking all that work would take him or her an entire day!)

How much will I make?

Once established, your housecleaning service will market itself in repeat and referral business. Allow about six months to get it going. Until then, plan on spending up to half of your time promoting your business and bidding on jobs.

Your overhead expenses will range from 25 to 50 percent of gross income, depending on the cost of your equipment and supplies. Taxes are included as well, though they vary depending on where you live.

How can I get started?

Start your housecleaning service by getting yourself organized for efficient cleaning. Gather the tools and materials you will need and learn how to use them efficiently. Next, produce a flyer that tells what you do, how much you charge, and how to contact you. Circulate it to potential customers.

Finally, look for ways to promote your business. Take your flyer to area home shows. Offer cleaning services to offices and small businesses. Give your brochures to friends and neighbors. Talk to someone at your local newspaper, giving them tips on cleaning that they can pass on to readers.

The SIC code for house and office cleaning is 7349-02.

How can I use computers to increase profits?

Housecleaning is low-tech. But high-tech computers can help track customers, promote your business, order supplies, and communicate with franchisors. In addition, computers can be used to share problems and solutions with other cleaning professionals via e-mail.

House-inspection service

What will I be doing?

If you have experience in the building trade and are looking for a profitable home-based business, consider starting a house-inspection service. This service involves the inspection of residential and commercial buildings for safety and compliance. Typically, if an individual is buying a home, he or she will have it inspected before the closing. As part of your service, you will make sure the plumbing, electrical wiring, and gas furnace are working and in compliance with codes. You may check the structure for evidence of termites or other pests. You'll climb into crawlspaces and attics. You'll check out the roof and foundations of the structure. In short, you'll assess the general condition of the building and point out any problems. You may also provide this service to building owners, insurance companies, bankers, or other clients interested in the condition of the structure.

What will I need to start?

To inspect structures, you must know what to look for. You'll need training and experience in the construction trade, in architecture, in electrical and/or plumbing systems, in heating systems, and related topics such as pests. You'll also need some tools such as an outlet tester, electrical tools, plumbing tools, pipe wrenches, screwdrivers, a ladder, and some flashlights. Your toolbox will be your best friend.

In addition to a local business license, your state or city may require a building inspector's license. Also consider professional trade certifications.

Who will my customers be?

Customers for your house-inspection service will include homeowners, homebuyers, lenders, real estate agents, investors, and insurance companies. Some house inspection services specialize in working with one type of client while others prefer more variety. A service in the Midwest specializes in working with local real estate agents who sell buyer assurance programs.

How much should I charge?

Home inspection takes time. A basic inspection may take just two hours and be priced at $100 while a thorough inspection with a fully documented report can take 8 hours and cost your customer $500 or more. Most inspection services fall in between, based on an hourly rate of $30 to $70.

How much will I make?

Overhead expenses for your house-inspection service include the costs of your home office, tools and equipment, transportation, and advertising. Estimate overhead at 15 to 40 percent of gross income. If you can bill 30 hours a week at $40 an hour (with 33 percent overhead), your net income will be about $40,000 a year.

How can I get started?

Besides knowing local construction requirements and regulations, you should also have extensive knowledge of pests, the local real estate marketplace, local lenders and insurance agents, and other resources. Learn whether you need a license or certification to be a

professional inspector. Find contacts within the local building industry that can help you find business and make incontestable inspections. Then get the word out to prospective customers through home
shows, service advertisements, and brochures. The American Society of Home Inspectors (800-243-2744) offers many resources, including the *ASHI Training Manual*.

The SIC code for house-inspection services is 6531-22.

How can I use computers to increase profits?

Home inspectors are paid for what they know about home construction, local building codes, real estate law, insurance law, and
about mortgages. One of the greatest tools for learning today is the
computer. It can be used to research thousands of subjects from home.
In addition, information that isn't online is typically in a book or
report that can be discovered and purchased online. Knowledge is
profit.

House-painting service

What will I be doing?

Painting is one of those jobs that most people don't like to do. It's
messy, it takes time, it's boring, and it means working on a ladder.
Not fun. If painting is fun to you—or at least something you're able
and willing to do quickly and efficiently—consider offering a house-
painting service. You may include homeowners as well as businesses
among your clients. And you may find yourself working indoors as
well as outdoors.

What will I need to start?

You should have experience in the trade. Maybe you've been a
painter and now want to work for yourself. Or maybe you've painted
so many of your own homes or apartments that your experience
level is high. Even so, read and practice more. You won't be paid as
much for your painting skills as your painting *efficiency*.

You'll need some equipment: a ladder, brushes and rollers, sprayer,
etc. You'll also need work clothing. In addition, you will need paints
and masking, but those can be purchased as you do the jobs.

Who will my customers be?

It's pretty easy to spot a potential customer for your exterior-
painting service. One successful painter simply drove through neighborhoods in the springtime, looking for houses that showed signs of

needing painting. He then gave a quote to the owner and suggested that he schedule all jobs by June 1 to ensure he could do them over the summer. In the fall he followed up with his exterior customers to find out if they needed interior painting over the winter months.

A small service ad in the local newspaper and your business card on area bulletin boards can help your potential customers identify themselves.

How much should I charge?

House painters get paid well. This is because of the skills and equipment they need as well as the fact that most people don't want to do the job themselves. The hourly rate for a house-painting service is $35 to $75. Most jobs are quoted by size or complexity once you estimate the time needed. Learn from each job, calculating what you should have charged and how to price more accurately in the future. For exterior jobs, some painters calculate the square footing on the main floor then multiply it by their pricing factor. If there is a second floor or dormers, the surface area to be painted is multiplied by a factor of 1.5 or 2 depending on how difficult it will be to paint. A smart painter drove around until he found a painting job in progress, where he stopped to interview the owner about pricing. A few calculations netted not only a fair pricing factor, but also guided him in setting his own hourly rate.

How much will I make?

Marketing your services will take much of your effort until you get a few jobs. Then you will probably be able to keep busy by spending 10 to 20 percent of your time looking for new jobs. If your pricing is reasonable and your work is good, referral business will do most of your marketing.

Overhead costs will range from 25 to 40 percent, depending on equipment and whether you include the cost of paint in your bid. Some quote a labor charge with paint and supplies extra.

How can I get started?

You must be more than a painter to succeed at this business. You must be an efficient painter. Develop your skills. Learn techniques that reduce time without reducing quality. Learn from each job you do. Buy quality equipment that will save you time in the long run. Let others know that you're in the house-painting business. Many customers will come to you.

Read *Painting Contractor: Start and Run a Money-Making Business* by Dan Ramsey (TAB/McGraw-Hill) available at *www.MulliganPress.com.*

The SIC code for house-painting services is 1721-01.

How can I use computers to increase profits?

Painting is labor-intensive. Painters typically use computers to track jobs and customers. They then use this information to develop new business and referrals. They send automatic mailings to customers 30 days after a job is done to ensure that they are still satisfied—and to gain a referral. Painters also use computer software to manage jobs and purchase materials.

House-sitting service

What will I be doing?

One of the easiest home-based jobs to start is a house-sitting service. As a house sitter, you'll be responsible for watching, checking on, or staying in vacant homes to minimize burglary or damage. Depending on the client's needs you may simply drive by once a day and pick up mail and newspapers—or actually stay in the home while the owners are gone. Beyond that basic service, you may feed and care for pets, water plants, check and forward telephone messages and important mail, and even clean the house.

What will I need to start?

House sitting requires no tools and few skills, but it does require honesty and a sense of trust. You may be required to be bonded and insured, depending on your clientele. Building a reputation as a trustworthy house sitter will build your business faster than paid advertising.

Some house sitters build a notebook of valuable information, which might include the names of customers and potential customers, emergency contacts for each, the location of hidden keys, codes for security systems, and more. You may also want a house-sitting kit that includes flashlights, household tools, notepads and pens, and other resources that may come in handy as you check out a home.

Who will my customers be?

In most cases, your customers will be homeowners and apartment dwellers who are traveling and will be away from their homes for more than a couple of days. Areas of more expensive homes may be a good area in which to start working.

Some house sitters specialize in vacant homes that are currently for sale or lease through local real estate companies. Contact agencies in your area to discuss their needs. Don't forget to contact bankers who may have repossessed homes that are vacant and need watching.

How much should I charge?

The hourly rate for house sitting is higher than you might imagine: $20 to $30. This is because watching a house really doesn't require much time. In fact, watching six nearby homes may take you less than an hour a day. If you are providing additional services (pet care, plant watering, lawn trimming, etc.), calculate your price based on your hourly rate. A weekly package that requires a total of two hours of your time can be fairly priced at $40 to $60 per week.

How much will I make?

You won't have to spend much time selling your services once established, typically 10 to 20 percent marketing time. Expenses are very low with overhead costs ranging from 15 to 25 percent Most important, work efficiently, plan your services, and offer value.

How can I get started?

There are probably many customers for your service already nearby. Once you've decided you want to build a house-sitting service, develop your product and your pricing, produce a flyer telling others about it and get it into circulation.

A smart house sitter took her first flyer to the local police department and asked to post it. If people calling in to notify police about going away on vacation asked, they were told about the house-sitting service and given a telephone number.

How can I use computers to increase profits?

How can a house sitter make more money by using a computer? Some house sitters are virtual. That is, they place sensors and motion detectors in the client's home that automatically send a message to the house sitter's pager if there is a problem. This lower-cost sitting service can be conducted while the house sitter is physically sitting another house. Amazing technology!

Inventory service

What will I be doing?

Computerized cash registers in stores not only add up the total of what you buy, they keep track of what has been sold. They manage the store's inventory and tell the owner what needs to be ordered. However, most stores still need to take what's called a physical inventory every few months to a year. This inventory is done by people who walk through the store, physically counting the numbers of each item on the shelves. If you have some experience doing this work, consider operating an inventory service from your home.

There are about 1,000 full-time inventory services in the United States—some hire independent contractors rather than employees. You can operate your business as an independent contractor or by hiring others to do the work.

What will I need to start?

Few skills are required for taking physical inventory. You must be accurate, conscientious, and careful. You can gain experience by offering your services to local retailers willing to train you. Depending on the type of inventory you manage, you may need hand-held computers or bar code scanners to count and keep track of items by product number. Sometimes the warehouse or retailer will provide these tools. But you may be able to earn a higher income if you supply your own.

Who will my customers be?

Your customers will be retail and wholesale businesses with inventory. Because businesses have different operating or fiscal years, the work may be year-round with high and low points. Your customers will identify when and why they need a physical inventory taken. Some proprietors of inventory services travel. One couple operates a successful service from a motor home. Clients are contracted a few months in advance. The couple arrives at the site, takes physical inventory, enjoys some time off in a new town, then moves on to the next contracted job.

How much should I charge?

Inventory services use an hourly rate of $25 to $50, depending on what tools they provide and their efficiency. Most price their service by the value of inventory or a flat per-day fee.

How much will I make?

Finding customers will take 10 to 20 percent of your time, leaving 80 to 90 percent billable. Overhead expenses range from 10 to 35 percent, depending on what you provide and whether you must travel to the inventory site. An inventory service can bring you a gross income of $30,000 to $75,000 a year with a net income of $20,000 to $55,000.

How can I get started?

The best way to learn this business is to do it for an employer. Look for inventory jobs in local newspapers. Ask friends who own businesses all you can about the inventory process and whether they take a physical inventory of stock. Finally, develop a flyer about your inventory service, including prices and experience, and circulate it to those who may need your services in the future. As you pass them out, ask businesses when they typically take physical inventory, then contact them about a month before that date. You may find yourself with a new customer.

The SIC code for inventory services is 7389-62.

How can I use computers to increase profits?

Today's inventory control is computerized. Instead of clipboards, inventory clerks punch in numbers or use scanner wands to identify and count inventory items. This information can then be downloaded into a notebook computer or sent as e-mail to a client or off-site inventory computer.

Janitorial service

What will I be doing?

The first janitors were doorkeepers and watchmen. As locks became more reliable, the castle's owners must have said, "Grab a broom!" and the predecessor to the modern janitor went to work.

Today, there are about 28,000 full-time janitorial services in the country, with many of them operating from homes across the nation. Most janitors serve the cleaning needs of businesses and stores. This is an especially important job in today's work environment where dirt particles can damage sensitive computers and other electronic equipment.

What will I need to start?

The skills required for cleaning are few. However, to clean efficiently requires training and experience. You can develop on-the-job experience by working as a janitor for a school or office, or as an employee of a successful janitorial service.

The equipment you'll need depends on the type of janitorial service you offer. Many janitorial services specialize in retail stores, offices, industrial buildings, warehouses, schools, hospitals, or other sites. Some services specialize in a type of cleaning such as floors, carpets, walls, and ceilings or glass cleaning. So defining what you do will help you determine what you need to start.

Fortunately, you can find much of the equipment and supplies you need at a single location: a wholesale janitorial supply store. In most cases, the supply store is operated by experienced janitorial service owners who can help you select equipment and supplies that are most efficient for what you do. Check area telephone books for janitorial suppliers.

Who will my customers be?

Your customers will be companies, individuals, municipalities, manufacturers, schools, hospitals, and others. One small janitorial service lost a major contract and needed to replace the income to pay for floor cleaning equipment just purchased. The owner decided to put the equipment to better use by specializing in stripping and waxing floors with a special polymer finish that offered both shine and durability. Within a couple of months she had replaced the income from the large account with numerous smaller accounts that gave her business more stability.

To find your customers, think like them. If you're thinking about starting a janitorial service for a specific retail area, talk to potential customers about their cleaning needs and schedules, how much they pay for janitorial services, and what it would take to earn their business. You may soon have your first customers lined up.

Some janitorial supply stores also work as job brokers, finding janitorial contracts and selling them to their customers. Ask supply stores if they also broker janitorial contracts.

How much should I charge?

The hourly rate for janitorial services is $25 to $60. However, most services quote prices based on the size of the job, frequency, and skills needed. Square footage is a common measurement. However, the price per square foot for floor care is quite different from that for emptying trash cans. Consider taking on a few jobs for a low hourly rate until you develop the skills and experience to work efficiently and know how best to price jobs.

How much will I make?

Once you've developed contract jobs, most of your time will be billable. Until then, plan to spend as much as 30 percent of your time marketing your janitorial service. How much will your overhead expenses be? They typically range from 20 to 40 percent, depending on the equipment required.

How can I get started?

The difference between a profitable janitorial service and one that is nearly bankrupt is, typically, knowledge. Learn your trade, develop skills, learn to work efficiently, and find out what your customers want. The more you know about your business and customers, the more successful and profitable your janitorial service will be.

The SIC code for janitorial services is 7349-02.

How can I use computers to increase profits?

Profitability in janitorial services means working efficiently. That means keeping track of customers, prospects, jobs, equipment, employees, and other tools. For years, these tools required manual records. Today's computer can help you track and schedule jobs, track bar-coded equipment, automatically notify employees, and more. It can also help you write job proposals.

Kennel

What will I be doing?

More than 12,000 kennels are now operated in the United States with the majority of them located on the same property where the owner lives. Running a kennel is an ideal home business.

There are many reasons why people use kennels: The owners are away for the weekend or for six months in Indonesia; the owner is in the hospital or nursing home for a short stay, or the animal must be quarantined in an approved facility for a few weeks.

What services do kennels offer? They provide lodging, food, and care to pets on behalf of their owners. Kennels take care of pets, typically dogs, on a short-term or long-term basis.

What will I need to start?

To start a kennel you must first know and love dogs. You don't have to be a veterinarian, but you will need to attend to the health needs of dogs in your care. You must recognize and sometimes treat health problems yourself.

Of course, you'll need a fenced kennel structure where you can keep the dogs. The more business you intend to seek, the larger the area you will need to house the dogs as well as to permit them space for exercise. You may also have facilities for cats or other pets, depending on your interests and local need. Designs for kennels are available in books on dog breeding and from kennel builders advertising in dog magazines. Of course, make sure your kennel complies with local zoning and health regulations.

One other thing you'll need: understanding neighbors. Don't try to set up a kennel in a residential neighborhood where barking will annoy people.

Who will my customers be?

Customers for your kennel include individuals with pets as well as companies and retailers. For example, one successful metropolitan kennel catered to area pet stores who needed a place to keep animals they had purchased but couldn't bring to the store, or animals under quarantine.

Most kennels offer services to the general public, working through local kennel clubs, advertising in newspapers and specialty publications, and by referral from animal shelters.

How much should I charge?

The hourly rate for kennels is difficult to calculate. You may charge an hourly rate for the time you are feeding and tending to the animals, and a daily rate for the kennel itself. You may even price your kennel by the size of the dog to reflect the additional room and food required.

A good way of setting your prices is to find out what others are charging in your area, then establishing your prices to draw business. This may mean lowering your price 10 to 20 percent or offering more services at the same price.

How much will I make?

How much your kennel will make depends on how well you can market it. Once established, your kennel should be able to give you a full-time income after paying all expenses. Overhead, once the kennel and equipment are purchased, will be 25 to 35 percent of gross income. Find ways of creatively marketing your kennel, or even breeding dogs yourself, to increase income and profits. Your gross income depends on what services you offer (feeding, exercise, training), what facilities you have (heated runs, indoor/outdoor kennel units) and how many units you have and keep full. If, for example, you have 20 units at $7 a day, and keep your kennel 75 percent full, your gross income will be about $38,000 a year. From this, deduct your overhead expenses to figure your net income ($25,000 to $29,000).

How can I get started?

Learn from others, develop skills working for others if possible, talk to prospective customers about their needs, plan your business on paper. This is especially true of kennels because so much depends on what you know. There are books on kennel management available through larger bookstores and dog breeder magazines. Contact your regional Small Business Administration office for more resources.

The SIC code for kennels is 0752-05.

How can I use computers to increase profits?

Computers offer a window to the world. You can advertise your kennel services on the Internet with your own Web page. You can correspond with other kennel owners and with customers. In addition, you can keep financial and customer records on your computer.

Kitchen remodeling

What will I be doing?

Here's an excellent home-based business idea for those who have a range of labor skills such as carpentry, painting, and cabinetmaking. It is also a profitable one. The kitchen is the most popular room for remodeling. A kitchen remodeler is paid for designing, refinishing, painting, and trimming kitchens and, sometimes, bathrooms. The kitchen remodeler has both the ideas and skills to modernize a kitchen to fit the needs and tastes of the homeowner.

What will I need to start?

To successfully remodel kitchens for profit, you must first know how to design kitchens for efficiency and beauty. Learn as much as you can about kitchens, popular kitchen designs, and materials and how to integrate them.

You'll need skills working with wood, cabinets, countertops, plumbing, electricity, paint, wallcoverings, flooring, and other components of the modern kitchen. Many people enhance these skills by working in the construction trade, especially for a professional remodeler. The more you know, the more you earn—and the fewer costly mistakes you make.

You will also need some tools and equipment as well as a vehicle for transporting them from job to job. You can have cabinets, countertops, and appliances delivered by your wholesaler so you don't need a large work truck. You can hire someone to pick up cabinets once you've removed them. Even the trunk of a car can serve as your toolbox. In it will be a power saw, hammers, screwdrivers, levels, measuring tapes, and other tools for installing cabinets, floors, and other materials.

Be sure to check with local and state licensing offices as you will probably need licensing and bonding to be a professional contractor.

Who will my customers be?

Customers for your kitchen remodeling business include individuals, contractors, and building material stores. An ad in the service directory of your local newspaper or in the area telephone book can help homeowners find you. General contractors may hire you for a job. Also, building material stores that sell cabinets and other kitchen fixtures may hire or recommend you for installation.

How much should I charge?

The rate for a kitchen remodeler varies from $30 to $75 an hour, but is priced by the job. Some kitchen remodelers use a markup of two or three times the cost of materials. Others price by the square foot size of the kitchen. A full kitchen remodel job will be priced from $3,000 to $10,000 or more depending on the size and quality of materials used for floors, cabinets, and countertops. A kitchen remodel can take from 20 to 60 hours depending on size, complexity, and whether you build your own cabinets or countertops.

How much will I make?

A successful kitchen remodeling business will require 15 to 30 percent of the owner's time for marketing and administration. The balance of time will be billable to customers. Overhead expenses, excluding the cost of materials, is typically 20 to 30 percent of income for telephone, advertising, licenses, a vehicle, etc. So a successful one-person kitchen remodeling business can earn a net income (before taxes) of $40,000 to $75,000 or more. Of course, it may take a year or two of hard work to get to this level, but many remodelers have done so.

How can I get started?

Kitchen remodelers are paid for their knowledge and efficiency. So, the more you know and the more efficiently you work, the more you will earn. To start your kitchen remodeling business, work for someone else developing your knowledge and skills. Build your toolbox. Take evening courses or read books on kitchen design. Study local building codes. Get the necessary contractor and business licenses. Find a job or two you can do to develop good references. Advertise where your competitors do.

The SIC code for kitchen remodelers is 1521-17.

How can I use computers to increase profits?

Sometimes the best way to sell a customer on a remodeling job is to show what it will look like when done. Computer Aided Design, or CAD software, can be used to both plan and illustrate kitchen remodeling jobs. In fact, using such software can make the job more efficient —and more profitable for you.

Landscaping service

What will I be doing?

Landscaping services do much more than just cut the grass. They are paid for designing, selecting, installing, and maintaining lawns, shrubs, and other landscape components. Some specialize in the design and hire contractors to do the dirty work while others prefer to get dirty rather than design. Those who do both well have greater potential for profits.

What will I need to start?

A landscaping service owner must have an extensive knowledge of plants and their care. He or she must know how to select hearty plants and keep them so. In some cases, a landscaping service is called in to correct problems.

To start a successful landscaping service you must be trained and experienced in the field. Most people in the business have developed experience working for someone else for at least five years. One season of cutting lawns isn't enough. Many in this trade have some formal or self-training in landscape design.

You may or may not need many tools for this business, depending on whether you expect to get dirty. Landscape designers can work with pencil and paper or computer. Installers and maintainers will need the standard array of tools: shovels, rakes and trimmers, as well as a lawnmower.

Who will my customers be?

Customers for your landscaping service include homeowners, apartment owners and managers, general contractors, retail businesses, manufacturers' offices, schools, and churches. If you have more experience working with one of these customer groups, focus on them until your business is built up. Of course, if there's already too much competition in your area for one type of customer, look to others.

How much should I charge?

Landscaping services set an hourly rate based on supply and demand. If there are many competitors, the supply may be high and prices lower. An alternative is to offer services that are in short supply and/or high demand. The typical rate is $30 to $75, priced by the value of the job and the time required. A simple landscape design requiring 10 hours may be priced at $500 while an annual maintenance contract of four hours a week can be priced at $8,000 or more.

How much will I make?

Like many service businesses, an established landscaping service can keep overhead expenses down by working from home and managing costs. In fact, overhead expenses (office, phone, advertising) should be about 25 to 35 percent of income. That means a successful one-person landscaping service can earn a net income for the owner of $30,000 to $60,000 or more a year.

How can I get started?

Many landscaping services start by working part-time on weekends to develop skills and customers, building into a full-time venture. Some offer limited services but spend any available time studying landscape design and related fields that will offer them greater income in the future.

Start by deciding what type of landscaping service you want to offer now, in two years and in five years. These are your goals. Then begin planning. Start gathering tools and equipment, learning what you need, looking for customers that fit those goals, and studying your competitors for opportunities to excel.

The SIC code for landscaping services is 0782-04.

How can I use computers to increase profits?

There are software programs on the market that can help you design, plan, and track landscaping jobs. Use one of the Internet search engines to look for "landscape planning software." Or read the ads in landscape trade publications for software. You can even find some lower-end software for landscape design at larger office supply businesses like Office Depot and OfficeMax.

Limousine service

What will I be doing?

Think of a limousine service as "a taxi service for the wealthy" and you will be wrong! Today's limousine service may transport a glittering star, but, on most days will be called on to carry newly-weds away from the church, impress a date, or even take a businessperson to the airport. Today's limousine services are creatively profitable.

A limousine service does more than drive people to specific locations. A taxi can do that. A limousine service does it with style. Your limousine service will take people where they want to go while treating them like royalty. Your limousine may provide a wet bar, snacks, or even a doorman along with a uniformed chauffeur.

Or not. One limousine service in the Midwest operates a shuttle service between the metro airport and the rural factory an hour away. It uses both stretch cars and passenger vans as needed. Successful? It has a fleet of six units under contract to the factory.

What will I need to start?

Of course, you need a "limousine," but you don't have to own it. You can rent one from a car rental agency or even another limo service as needed. Or you can lease one. Sometimes you can purchase an older unit from a service in a nearby metro area.

You will also need a working knowledge of the area you serve. However, unlike the taxi business, you typically have time to refer to maps and even drive a route if needed before picking up your client. In addition, you may need a chauffeur's uniform or at least a business suit and cap.

You'll probably need a license and special insurance much like that required of taxi services. Contact your regional Small Business Administration office for specific requirements in your area.

Who will my customers be?

Customers for your limousine service will be individuals and businesses. Individuals will hire you for weddings, anniversaries, parties, special events, and simply for fun. Businesses may hire you as an airport transporter, to pick up important clients or to deliver a salesperson for a lasting impression.

How much should I charge?

Limousine services set a rate of $35 to $70 an hour, but typically price by the mile or time and mileage. A wedding package of two hours may be priced at $100, while taking four executives to the airport may be priced at 35 cents each mile per person. In some areas, local tariffs will dictate what you can charge.

How much will I make?

Expenses can be high for an idle limo. So how much your service makes will depend on how well you market it. Be creative. An Arizona limousine service doesn't use standard stretch limos—it uses classic cars. By doing so, it provides a unique service that markets itself. The cars are also rented as needed to motion picture film companies working in the area.

If you do many of your own repairs, keep home office expenses down and market smart, your limousine service can offer you a net income (after overhead) of $25,000 to $45,000 a year or more.

How can I get started?

This is one business where market research is especially important. If this is the business you want to start at home, begin your research today. Find out who your competitors will be, how much they charge, whether any of them are profitable (or bankrupt) and who they serve. Then look for potential customers. If you plan to focus on wedding parties, talk to local wedding counselors about the opportunities and maybe even some shared marketing.

Once your market is defined you can better decide whether to buy, lease, rent, or borrow a limo. Start small and slowly work toward a booming business.

The SIC code for limousine services is 4119-03.

How can I use computers to increase profits?

How can travelers looking for airport or limousine services find you? One place is in the telephone book. Another is on the Internet.

Once you have a basic Web site (with your own e-mail address), ask other local businesses to "trade links" or list their Web site on yours and vice versa. In addition, add your Web address and e-mail address to your business cards.

Manufacturer

What will I be doing?

Do you like putting things together and trying to figure out a more efficient and faster way to do it? If so, consider a manufacturing business in your home. A manufacturer doesn't have to have an immense building and hundreds of workers. You can be a manufacturer in a spare room or the garage. A manufacturer is someone who makes a product from a variety of materials. You can be a dress manufacturer turning cloth into clothing. You can be a toy manufacturer assembling children's toys from parts you buy from another manufacturer. Best of all, you can do it at home.

What will I need to start?

Manufacturing is such a broad category that it's difficult to tell you exactly what you'll need to start your business at home. The best place to start is with a product. For example, you can manufacture executive pen sets. You'll need to find a source for the pens, the bases, felt for the base bottom, some trim pieces and maybe a plaque that can be engraved depending on who is buying the sets. Sources for materials in this example include pen manufacturers, trophy supply wholesalers, felt wholesalers, etc.

You may need some manufacturing equipment, depending on what you're making. There are two approaches to getting started in manufacturing. Either get specialized equipment that minimizes your competition, or simple equipment that minimizes your initial investment.

Who will my customers be?

Depending on what you're manufacturing, your customers may be retailers, wholesalers, other manufacturers, or even consumers. Many small home-based manufacturers start by selling to consumers and retailers until their product and system are refined, then they sell to wholesalers or other manufacturers when they can deliver larger quantities.

Reaching your defined customers means calling on them with your product in hand. This is true if you're selling to consumers, retailers, wholesalers, or manufacturers. Be prepared to sell what you make. Who better to represent your business than you?

How much should I charge?

This is a tough question to answer. Small manufacturers, once established, typically use a rate of $40 to $80 an hour to calculate pricing. However, most soon set prices by percentage of value of manufactured product. For example, a manufacturer of pen sets may calculate that 30 percent of the wholesale price he charges will go for his labor, 50 percent for materials, and 20 percent for overhead expenses.

How much will I make?

An established small manufacturer can earn an income of $15,000 to $75,000 a year, depending on many factors including demand for the product, manufacturing efficiency, marketing skills, and the ability to find the least expensive sources for materials and supplies you will need. Start small, learn from every mistake, and don't expand until you have it down right. Equipment maintenance can be a big expense in manufacturing, so be sure and take that into consideration when estimating your overhead expenses.

How can I get started?

The best place to start a small manufacturing business is not with a product but with a customer. Depending on your skills, you may find a local wholesaler who can sell a specific type of product for you. Or you may find a retail chain that needs hanging planters, for example. Calculate whether you can manufacture them profitably. If so, get a written order, buy materials and equipment and get to work. You'll soon learn what you do best, how to make it profitable, and where to sell it in the future.

How can I use computers to increase profits?

Manufacturing means inventory. The most efficient way of tracking and managing inventory is with computer software. Inventory databases and spreadsheets can help you know exactly what you have, how much it cost, how much you can profitably sell it for, and how fast it is selling. And by setting up a Web site you can sell your inventory via the Internet.

Masonry service

What will I be doing?

Concrete and brick are all around us. The people who install them are called masons or mason contractors. There are more than 11,000 full-time masonry contractors in the United States. Masonry services design, install and maintain, concrete, brick, rock, and other masonry products. These products come in many forms: buildings, fences, walls, sidewalks, and other structures. If you have proven your masonry skills working for someone else, maybe it's time to consider working for yourself.

What will I need to start?

Masons need extensive skill and training for many jobs. However, other jobs, such as installing a brick or concrete walkway, can be done by the novice. You will only be able to sell the skills you have, so the first step to starting a masonry service is measuring your current skills and experience.

The second step is to gather tools and equipment you'll need. If you're repairing sidewalks, for example, you'll need a concrete mixer and concrete hand tools. If you're building block walls, you'll need mortar equipment and tools.

Who will my customers be?

As an employed mason, you probably didn't have to worry about who your customers were. Your customer was your foreman. You did what the foreman said and everybody was happy. But as you market your masonry skills, you must first determine who to sell to.

Customers for your masonry service depend on what services you offer. In most cases, your customers will be general contractors, remodeling contractors, homeowners, apartment owners, retail businesses, office building owners, and manufacturing plants. Fortunately, once identified, they can be contacted through listings in local telephone books or through regional associations.

How much should I charge?

The rate for a masonry service varies greatly by skills, but typically ranges from $40 to $80 an hour. Subcontracted work is typically priced by the hour. However, many jobs are bid by the size and complexity of the job. A masonry wall might be priced by the block or the surface. A concrete walk or driveway would be priced by the square foot and the thickness in inches. Some trades will have locally standardized pricing with little variation while other areas are more competitive.

How much will I make?

You'll find that 20 to 30 percent of your time will be spent looking for jobs. This will be reduced once you establish yourself and start getting repeat and referral business. However, it may be higher as you begin your business.

Overhead expenses will range from 20 to 40 percent of income. A masonry job may give you $600 after paying for materials. But of that, $120 to $240 will go for equipment, tools, office expenses, and taxes. A full-time masonry service can earn $25,000 to $60,000 a year or more.

How can I get started?

Masonry is a trade. How much training and experience you will need depend on what type of work you do. A terrazzo mason may require 20 years of trade experience before starting a contracting business. A sidewalk installer may need only two years of experience.

Start gathering your tools. You will probably have many of them, but not the more expensive ones like mixers and tampers. You will also need the tools you will use in your office: telephone, fax, maybe a computer.

If you're currently employed as a mason, watch for an opportunity to discuss your goals with your employer. Do so carefully, because some employers may consider you a potential competitor and fire you on the spot. Others will welcome a known subcontractor and help you get your start.

The SIC code for masonry services is 1741-01.

How can I use computers to increase profits?

A mason is a craftsperson. Making money at the craft requires maintaining records of jobs, customers, materials, and equipment. Computers can make the job easier with database software, customer contact software, and profitability spreadsheets. Computers give masons more time to ply their craft profitably.

Pet groomer

What will I be doing?

If you enjoy dogs, consider joining the nearly 20,000 full-time pet grooming shops in the United States, many of which work from their home. A pet groomer offers services such as washing, trimming, and grooming dogs, cats, and other pets for owners. Learnable skills are required, as is a concern and interest for the health, beauty, and temperament of these animals.

What will I need to start?

To be a professional pet groomer you must have knowledge and training in a variety of areas. There are schools, books, videos, and other resources for learning these skills. The best is on-the-job experience. If you don't already have experience, get it now by working in a pet grooming shop in your area.

To offer pet grooming services you'll need a convenient location where people can bring their animals for care. If your home is difficult to find, consider making your business mobile and going to your customers. You can set up shop in a travel trailer or mobile home that visits your customers.

You'll also need some tools (clippers, trimmers, etc.) and supplies (shampoos, detanglers, flea sprays, etc.). Most pet groomers also carry pet-grooming products to sell to customers—much as a beauty shop carries a line of beauty aids.

Who will my customers be?

Customers for your pet-grooming services include pet owners, veterinarians, and pet stores. If you have many potential competitors, look for a unique service or unserved customers that you can build your business around. For example, specialize in caring for dogs that most groomers don't like to handle. Using safe restraining equipment, you can serve these specialized customers and probably get a higher price than for grooming most dogs. Or consider specializing in services for older dogs or even for cats. They don't all groom themselves!

How much should I charge?

The rate for a pet groomer is $35 to $45 an hour, priced by service and size of pet. Shampoos for dogs weighing more than 20 pounds, for example, will be priced higher than for those under that weight. The price for a package of services will be lower than for a single service because you can work more efficiently. To find out what your competitors are charging, start calling around for rates.

How much will I make?

There is no record of anyone getting filthy rich as a pet groomer—just filthy. Even so, you can make a modest income. An established pet-grooming service can bill for about six hours a day with an overhead cost of 25 to 50 percent, depending on equipment. So a one-person pet-grooming service can earn a net income of $25,000 to $45,000 a year before taxes.

How can I get started?

You can develop your pet-grooming skills on your own pets and with some training, but try to work at a groomer's shop for at least a year. Along the way, gather your tools and equipment.

Consider locating your pet-grooming shop in your garage or home. A utility room may have the needed plumbing and electrical service for your grooming area. Of course, make sure that local zoning allows you to operate this business from your home.

Join local dog and pet associations, advertise in local newspapers and phone books and tell your friends and neighbors. Once you've developed a steady clientele, your pet grooming service will be a fun and profitable home business.

The SIC code for pet groomers is 0752-04.

How can I use computers to increase profits?

Pet groomers don't have time to keep good records. An appointment book is all most of them use. The more profitable ones also use a computer to not only track appointments, but also customers, individual pets, costs, and profits. This information is used to fill out the appointment book on slow days, to sell related products and services based on customer needs, and to help personalize service.

Picture-framing service

What will I be doing?

Photos and drawings are enhanced by a quality frame. If you enjoy working with art or with wood and other materials, consider a home-based picture-framing service, designing, selecting, constructing, and installing frames on art, photographs, and documents. Such a business can be operated in or from your home, serving a wide variety of customers.

What will I need to start?

To start your picture-framing service you'll first need training or experience in selecting and installing frames. You can get this experience working for a framing shop or by studying books on framing, and by practicing on your own frames.

A framer typically works at a framing table with clamps, saws, and other tools of the trade. For efficiency, you may need an air compressor to power a pneumatic stapler or other tool. Materials and supplies are available in wholesale framing catalogs and stores found in most metropolitan telephone books.

Who will my customers be?

Customers for your picture-framing service include individuals, artists, other businesses, and wholesalers. Some framers prefer to work directly with the public while others don't. In most areas, you have a choice. One successful framer has four galleries as clients, all located in a resort town. She visits the shops once a week to pick up any art that requires a frame or frame repair, bringing it back the next week. Another framer specializes in ornate frames for awards and certificates, selling his products to wholesalers.

Once you've defined who your customers are and what they want, it will be easier to find them through mailing lists and advertising.

How much should I charge?

Framing services typically establish a shop rate of $30 to $60 an hour, but price by the size of the frame, the complexity of the project, and the quality of materials. A frame that requires 20 minutes to construct and install at $45 an hour means $15 in labor. Add materials at retail prices (two to three times wholesale) to establish the frame's price. Depending on clientele, you may be able to increase the price based on perceived value of the frame.

How much will I make?

Once established, marketing and administration for your framing service will require about 20 to 30 percent of your time. If you have minimal tools, your overhead will be about 25 percent of income, while a fully equipped shop may take up to 50 percent, including taxes. A full-time framing service can net the owner $30,000 to $60,000 a year.

How can I get started?

First, learn your trade. Develop knowledge and skills for framing through working in a frame shop or taking an adult education class on framing. Next, create your own flyer and circulate it to potential customers. You can pass it out at art shows, at artist's club meetings and to friends and neighbors. Also tell your local newspapers about your new business, offering them something newsworthy.

The SIC code for picture-frame dealers is 5999-27; for framing services it's 7699-15.

How can I use computers to increase profits?

Picture framing is a craft business. As such, many picture framers operate from home and rely on UPS to deliver and ship products. That means that the entire world is your customer. Of course, you're competing with other picture framers—unless you offer something unique. Then you can promote your uniqueness with your own Web site and sell your services wherever the brown UPS truck goes.

Pool cleaning

What will I be doing?

Anyone who has owned a pool or spa knows how much work cleaning it can be. It seems like a pool needs to be constantly checked and adjusted. If you have experience caring for pool systems, consider a home-based pool cleaning and maintenance service.

What will I need to start?

Equipment for cleaning pools and spas will vary from floating cleaners to skimmers and chemicals. You will probably need a pickup truck or small van to carry your equipment and supplies.

Most important, you'll need training and experience with pool maintenance. While there are books and videos on the subject, nothing replaces hands-on experience. If this is a business you would enjoy but you don't have enough training, consider working for a large pool maintenance service for awhile to develop knowledge and skills.

Who will my customers be?

Most of your customers will be homeowners and apartment complex owners with private swimming pools. In some cities, pool owners can be found by checking the county tax assessor's records. You can also offer pool maintenance services to public pools or to gymnasiums. You can try to find your customers through public records or you can advertise your services in local newspapers and let your customers find you, or you can do both.

How much should I charge?

The hourly rate for pool cleaning and maintenance depends somewhat on equipment, services provided, and the competition in your area. However, many set prices based on an hourly rate of $30 to $50, then charge by the month or season. A weekly maintenance check and monthly cleaning requiring a total of two hours a month can be priced at $60 to $100 a month, depending on your hourly rate.

How much will I make?

Pool cleaning and maintenance is typically done under a contract with the pool owner. So once your contracts are written, you can concentrate on your work rather than selling. Until then, plan to spend up to one-third of your time marketing your business. Your overhead expenses will range from 20 to 40 percent of income, depending on whether you supply chemicals or the customer does. In fact, some pool-cleaning services have two prices based on whether they furnish required chemicals. Even so, they may be the one to sell the chemicals to the pool owner, so additional profits are possible.

A full-time home-based pool cleaning service can bring in a net income of $40,000 to $60,000 a year or more before taxes.

How can I get started?

The National Pool and Spa Association offers training aids for pool-maintenance workers and businesses. Also, get on-the-job training as an employee of a pool service, or at least with your own or a neighbor's pool. Let others know about your service by developing a flyer that describes the benefits of what you do and why you are the best choice for pool service. Give prospects a reason to call you—a free pool checkup would be a good incentive.

The SIC code for pool cleaning and maintenance is 7389-09.

How can I use computers to increase profits?

Pools aren't your customers. People are. To efficiently track and sell customers, use computer software to maintain customer records and to do your billing. Consider using your computer to send out monthly mailings to regular customers asking for referrals, offering special deals, reselling past customers, and other promotional efforts. Publish a newsletter.

Recycling service

What will I be doing?

Recycling has become big business. As much as 50 percent of materials in some automobiles come from recycled materials. Other products also depend on recycled materials, which are often recycled for profit.

For example, one recycler was a man who stopped at furniture stores once a week to haul away the boxes that dinettes and chairs were shipped in. He did the store a service at no charge, disassembling the boxes so they lay flat in the back of his pickup truck. Once he had a full load, he took it to a cardboard recycler in a nearby city where he sold the load by weight.

What will I need to start?

To recycle for profit, you must know something about the needs of your customers and buyers. Many customers will give you the materials in exchange for hauling them away.

You'll probably need some way of transporting what you recycle. Many recyclers use a pickup truck or an open trailer pulled by a car. For smaller items, the trunk of a sedan may offer enough storage until your business gets off the ground. An enterprising recycler started his business by walking along rural roads as self-appointed litter patrol, picking up cans and bottles that offered a return on deposit.

Who will my customers be?

Your customers will be wholesale recyclers. These are the folks that will buy your materials for recycling. To find wholesale recyclers, check area telephone books under recycling and related headings, depending on what you will be collecting: cans, bottles, scrap metal, glass, paper, cardboard, plastics, or all of the above.

How much should I charge?

You will be paid by your ability to find profitable materials for recycling. At first, your efforts to recycle may only earn $10 to $15 an hour. Once you've found materials in greater demand and a market for them, you should be able to earn $25 to $45 an hour. Most recycled materials are resold by the pound, based on fluctuating local market conditions.

With experience, you'll also get better at estimating material value, at negotiating, and at knowing current market value of materials. You may also find additional customers for your materials, giving you alternate places to sell.

Overhead expenses directly relate to your costs to transport materials from your resources to your customers. If you already own a pickup or a car and open trailer, initial expenses will be less.

How much will I make?

Your price may vary. How much you will make as a recycler depends much on what you know, what you do, and for whom you do it. A full-time recycler can make a net income of $25,000 to $40,000 a year. Some do even better.

How can I get started?

The best way to start a recycling service is to start learning what you can about it. Call recyclers in the telephone book. Check with municipal and state offices for government resources and guidelines. Ask people you know about recycling and whether they have any resources or contacts.

Next, select a customer for selling your materials for recycling by contacting businesses in your area that use materials that can be recycled. Then find resources for these materials. Finally, start gathering materials for recycling and begin the learning process.

The SIC code for recycling service businesses is 5093-12.

How can I use computers to increase profits?

Recycled materials (glass, aluminum, paper, etc.) are commodities just like oil and wheat. As such, they are sold to the highest bidder. Use your computer to learn about the regional and even national market for recycled materials. You may find that you can get a better price nearby. Use your computer to research the market for recycled materials—and increase your profits.

Rental manager

What will I be doing?

What kind of home business can you start if you don't have a home? You can be an on-premise rental manager, responsible for collecting rents, maintaining security, interviewing prospective renters, and even maintaining the property for owners of apartments or commercial buildings. The greater your responsibility, the more you will be paid.

Many rental managers are independent contractors, although some have an employee relationship with the rental property. Some enterprising folks work as a rental manager and, in their spare time, operate another home-based business.

What will I need to start?

To be a good rental manager you must be a people person. You must know how to get along with nearly anyone, and how to handle the others. It will also be useful to know basic maintenance skills such as minor plumbing repairs, painting, and related tasks. Of course, you should be trustworthy. Your employer may require that you are bonded if you collect rent money. You should be able to keep good records and make bank deposits for the building owners. You should also know the local tenants' rights laws that you will have to comply with.

Who will my customers be?

Your customers will be investment property owners that you can find through newspaper ads, real estate offices, and other sources. One enterprising woman was a live-in rental manager for a large complex but also served as on-call manager for a smaller complex nearby and two storage rental units a few miles away. All of her employers approved of the arrangement because she was trustworthy, efficient, and a hard worker.

How much should I charge?

It's difficult to set an hourly rate for rental managers because, most of the time, you're on-call. Instead, your income can come from a salary or a percentage of rents and an hourly fee for maintenance work.

How much will I make?

A rental manager can get free rent, a salary, maintenance wages, and other income that can come to $2,000 a month or more. Depending on your responsibilities, you may also be able to operate a noncompeting home-based business when you're not on duty.

How can I get started?

Start reading the ads for rental managers in area newspapers to learn what is typically required. Look for opportunities to combine jobs to increase your income. Contact local investment real estate agents. Call state and local government offices to find out what rights tenants and landlords have in your area. Start building your set of references to show to prospective customers. Use your own experiences as a renter to convince property owners that you will manage their rentals well.

How can I use computers to increase profits?

Rental management means a lot of recordkeeping. Computers can help by tracking units, renters, applications, maintenance, income, and expenses. The rental owners may supply the computer or you can use your own. You can e-mail them monthly reports to keep them informed and you can even build a Web site to promote your rental units to keep occupancy high.

Saw-sharpening service

What will I be doing?

Nearly every home has a saw blade, lawnmower blade, scissors, knife, or other utensil that needs sharpening. The problem is that most folks list "sharpening" as their 47th priority until they use the blade or until a saw-sharpening service reminds them.

That's where you come in. Your saw-sharpening service can keep blades and tools sharp and safe for your customers as you make money at home.

What will I need to start?

Sharpening is a skill that can be learned. It will take some studying and practice, but you can develop this skill in just a few weeks. If you already know the basics of sharpening, you're ahead of the game. Books available through larger bookstores and libraries will show you how. Highly recommended is Don Geary's *How to Sharpen Anything* (TAB Books).

You will also need tools. Which ones? That depends on what you will be sharpening. While a bench grinder/sharpener is your first tool, there are other stationary power tools better suited to sharpening saw blades and related edged tools. You can find these tools in larger tool catalogs and industrial supply houses listed in phone books.

Who will my customers be?

Who will hire you to sharpen blades? That depends on the blades. For example, saw blades are sharpened for building contractors and woodworkers. Knife blades can be sharpened for professional cooks and meat cutters. Lawnmower blades can be sharpened for lawncare businesses, lawnmower shops, and individuals. Some sharpening services are under contract to local wood mills or other manufacturers to keep their blades sharpened.

How much should I charge?

The shop rate for a saw shop is $30 to $60 an hour, but most services are priced by the unit. Sharpening a 10-inch circular blade may take 20 minutes of your time including setup. If your shop rate is $30 an hour, the price can be $10 (one-third of the hourly rate). However, if you have little competition and there is a great need for your services, consider charging 10 to 20 percent more. Then, during slow periods you can cut your price to draw business when you need it more.

How much will I make?

Saw sharpening and filing services can earn the owner a very good net income once the business is built and all equipment is working efficiently. Some sharpening equipment is automated and will allow you to handle two or more jobs at once, increasing your income. What can you do when business is slow? One enterprising saw-sharpening business bought used blades at garage sales and from industrial salvagers, then sharpened and sold them when business was slow. The hourly rate was lower than for other jobs, but it was better than nothing. Annual net income for a sharpening service ranges from $25,000 to $55,000.

How can I get started?

There are numerous books, courses, classes, videos and other training aids for those who want to learn how to sharpen saws and other blades. Equipment manufacturers also offer instructions. If you need experience, buy up used blade tools and practice on them.

Remember that sharpening blades is a low priority for most consumers, so you will have to keep reminding them that you are in business to serve this need. Place a small ad in local telephone books and service directories. If you can, make sure your home-based shop has a large sign identifying your services (many neighborhoods don't allow this so check with local zoning first). Even go door-to-door if you must to find new business.

The SIC code for saw-sharpening services is 7699-24.

How can I use computers to increase profits?

Small businesses like saw-sharpening services don't offer much time for keeping books. So many of these businesses rely on simple bookkeeping programs like Quicken or Money to manage records. Saw sharpening is a service business with little or no inventory, so the record system is simple. A basic integrated program like Microsoft Works can handle the database, spreadsheet, word processing, and other tasks.

Security service

What will I be doing?

It's an insecure world. Individuals and businesses feel threatened by crime. You can help them be more secure by offering your services. A security service designs and manages security systems for individuals and businesses. One security system may install and monitor alarm systems while another provides bodyguard protection. A third security service may help architects design buildings that minimize security problems.

What will I need to start?

To offer this service, you must be an expert in your field of security. Once you decide on a field of expertise, develop your knowledge and experience in that field. If you want to offer a security guard service, for example, find employment in the field and get on-the-job training.

Some security services require knowledge of electronic equipment installation and use. You may sell and install burglar alarm systems in homes or stores. Or you may have an audio monitoring system in your home that allows you to listen in at homes where the owners are away.

In some fields of security you will need licensing and bonding. In others you may require training in electronics or in self- defense.

Who will my customers be?

Who will hire you? That depends on what services you provide and who will most benefit. If you enjoy guarding valuable materials, offer a bonded guard service to businesses where crime has been a problem. If you will specialize in designing and installing security systems, your customers will be those who have had break-ins at or near their home or business. Reading police reports in the newspaper or at the police department will help you find your potential customers.

How much should I charge?

The rate for security services varies between $25 to $60 an hour depending on what services are offered and how specialized they are. Some security systems price systems by size while guard services typically charge by the shift, the week, or the month. A security system can be priced based on the square footage of the area it secures.

Find out what your local competitors charge for similar services and you will have a starting point for pricing your services to be competitive.

How much will I make?

After a year of operation, your security business should be able to bill for 80 to 90 percent of available time. Overhead expenses will range from 20 to 50 percent depending on whether you hire employees to do some of the work. An established security system can net the owner $30,000 to $60,000 a year.

How can I get started?

First, select a group of potential customers who have security problems. They may be people in a specific neighborhood or retail shopping district or industrial park. Next, decide what products and services you can offer to make them more secure. It may be a patrol service, an alarm installation service, an alarm leasing service, or a combination of services. Finally, interview potential customers to learn how they feel about security, whether they have unmet needs, and what they are now paying for security services or would be willing to pay.

Contact the International Association of Professional Security Consultants (301-913-0030).

The SIC code for security services is 7381-02.

How can I use computers to increase profits?

Today's security industry is about electronics. Computers have immensely helped make people more secure. Though you may only use PCs for record-keeping, you should learn more about computers and how they are used in the security industry to monitor, identify, and secure locations. Also search the Web for new information on how computers can make you more money.

Sign service

What will I be doing?

You don't have to be an artist to operate a successful home-based sign service. In fact, you can learn your trade as you go. A sign service designs, produces, and/or sells signs to advertise and inform. If you're artistic you can design unique signs for businesses, churches, or other groups. If you're not artistic, you can construct signs from designed components. If you're not good at assembling things, you can sell preproduced signs.

Of course, the more skills you have, the more you will be paid. But you can start small and build your skills as you build your home business.

What will I need to start?

Before you start your sign service, take an inventory of your skills and experience. Here are some options: Design and draw unique business signs; repair or restore older signs; produce or repair neon signs; purchase and resell stock signs available from wholesalers; or subcontract your services to a regional sign installer.

In each type of business, your startup requirements are different. So decide what sign services you can best offer and start planning how you will offer them. You may need a commercial vehicle to transport signs, or tools for shaping glass tubes for neon sign—or you may need jigs to specialize in producing wooden signs.

Who will my customers be?

Your customers are all around you. Start looking today for the types of businesses and groups that most frequently use the signs you will be selling or servicing. You may decide to specialize in restoring signs in older shopping areas or in producing stylistic signs for upscale businesses. As you drive around, look for such signs and potential customers.

One man found himself in the sign business when he bought a box at an auction. In the box were hundreds of stock signs that said "Open/Closed," "Employees Only," "Restrooms," and other common signs. He loaded them in the trunk of his car and drove along a nearby highway looking for small businesses. If he spotted one with poor signs he stopped and showed his wares. In less than a month he had built sufficient capital to start a sign service employing others to do the same.

How much should I charge?

Your hourly rate will depend on your creativity. If you're selling stock signs, your rate will be much lower than if you are designing and producing unique signs. A typical rate is $30 to $60 an hour, depending on needed skills and tools. Once installed, you can contract with the sign owner for ongoing maintenance.

How much will I make?

Income for a sign service is as varied as the signs provided. In general, however, 25 to 50 percent of sales income will go to cover overhead expenses including telephone, advertising, and equipment. Of course, your own sign won't cost you much. If your neighborhood doesn't allow signage, find out if you can park your business vehicle in front of your home with a sign on the side of it.

How can I get started?

Learn your trade. If you are simply selling stock signs, learn the skills of salesmanship. If you will be producing neon signs, take courses, and get a job doing so for an employer before you start your business.

Gather your tools. You will need tools and equipment for most types of sign services, including a vehicle to transport signs or your tools. Start finding the tools you need and the best way to transport and use them.

Look for opportunities. Consider starting by refurbishing existing signs. It can help you develop your skills, your income, and your customers.

Subscribe to *Sign Business Magazine* (303-469-0424).

The SIC code for sign services is 3993-02 and for sign painters is 7389-05.

How can I use computers to increase profits?

Computers have revolutionized sign making. There are now software programs that will not only guide you in designing signs, but will also guide an attached printer in printing it. Not just small signs, but also large vinyl lettering that can be affixed to solid signage. Check sign trade journals for information and ads on the latest software packages for sign shops.

Tailor

What will I be doing?

There are about 12,000 full-time tailors in the United States. A tailor makes, alters and enhances clothing for others. If you have the skills and the experience to offer these services, consider starting your own tailor service.

What will I need to start?

Besides skills in alterations and clothing making, tailors also need to know how to work with customers. One tailor specializes in helping executives. She goes to the executive's office for the fitting and, once done, delivers the custom-tailored clothing to the office.

If you have experience in this trade, you probably already have the tools you'll need. Many tailors have a second set of basic tools they use on the road.

Who will my customers be?

Customers for your tailor service include individuals, clothing resellers, and alteration shops. You can specialize in suits, for example, and offer your services to alteration shops that may not have anyone on staff to do the work.

How much should I charge?

The typical rate for tailors is $25 to $60 an hour, depending on skills, experience, and name value. Many tailors price by service or by a percent of garment value. The percent will depend on the complexity of the garment and the skills needed for the tailoring. Alterations will earn a lower rate, while clothing design earns a higher fee.

How much will I make?

An established tailor will spend just 10 to 20 percent of his or her time marketing the business. Overhead expenses are lower than many businesses, ranging from 10 to 25 percent. Being able to work from your home gives you an advantage over tailor shops that must pay rent on a retail store.

How can I get started?

Contact local clothiers and alteration shops, letting them know of your experience and your rates. Some may already have a tailor, but may need to call another one for rush jobs or overload work. Give them your business card and flyer.

Find ways to publicize your business in local newspapers and other media. If you have tailored clothing for the rich and famous or for people in another country, turn this interesting information into a feature story that can help you build local credentials and get you noticed.

The SIC code for tailors is 5699-19.

How can I use computers to increase profits?

Tailors are craftspeople. Computers can't help with the craft, but they can help run the business. Most small businesses benefit from accounting and other business software. Tailors can, too. They can also use desktop publishing software to make signs, alteration tickets, sales forms, rate sheets, brochures, and other valuable business tools.

Tree-trimming service

What will I be doing?

A tree-trimming service does just what the name implies: trims trees. Tree trimmers are called to remove limbs or trees that are diseased or damaged. They also remove limbs close to power, cable, and telephone lines. They are called to remove trees that have fallen on to a house or in to a road. Their service is important and their income is good.

What will I need to start?

To offer a tree-trimming service you obviously must know something about trees, how they grow, and how to remove or stop growth. Community colleges and universities with agriculture departments can direct you to courses and books on these subjects.

To gain experience, practice on your own trees or, better, work part- or full-time for a tree-trimming or landscaping service. The experience you gain will later make you more money. If you have knowledge but need practice, offer to trim trees for friends, neighbors, churches, and others who love your price: free.

Your equipment will include a chain saw, tree saws, cutters, trimmers, and related equipment as well as ladders and maybe a climbing belt. Wear goggles, a safety hat, and other safety gear so you can enjoy your business for many years.

Who will my customers be?

Customers for your tree-trimming service are easy to find. Simply drive neighborhoods and business districts looking for trees that need your services, then contact the owner. One trimmer took photos of problem trees and brought them to the owner with a suggestion on how to solve the problem. In many cases, the solution sounded like too much work to the owner and the trimmer was hired to do it.

Windstorms can play havoc on trees and limbs. Listen to regional news and, if a windstorm hits a neighboring area, get there fast. Offer your services to area tree trimmers, insurance agents, disaster relief offices, or individual homeowners. Stop by City Hall first and make sure you have the proper licenses for the area.

How much should I charge?

Tree-trimming services set rates of $35 to $60 an hour in most areas, depending on equipment, efficiency, and competition. If all you have is a ladder and a saw, your rate will be on the lower end of the scale. A pickup truck with a "cherry picker" hydraulic bucket and power saws will get the higher rates for the more sophisticated jobs.

To fill in time between emergency jobs and driving neighborhoods, offer tree maintenance services. Once a month, you will check and trim trees for an apartment or business complex. Your fee will be slightly lower than standard because you will have an annual contract that guarantees some income. How you charge for this service depends on what you do.

How much will I make?

A tree-trimming service can give you $30,000 to $60,000 in gross income each year. Deducting overhead expenses of 25 to 50 percent for advertising, telephone, equipment, office supplies, and inevitable taxes, gives you a good income at what can be an enjoyable job.

How can I get started?

Learn as much as you can about trees and how to efficiently maintain them. Practice your skills on your own trees or others, carefully discovering the best tools and techniques for the job. Let others know about your services and their benefits. Produce a flyer with pricing. Order and distribute business cards. Talk with others about trees and how to maintain them. Let people know you're an expert.

Enjoy what you do. Enjoyment breeds enthusiasm in you as well as your customers.

The SIC code for tree-trimming services is 0783-01.

How can I use computers to increase profits?

Tree trimmers can easily work from home and a work vehicle. Consider producing advertising fliers and distributing them in neighborhoods in which you have a job. Also use them to canvas for potential customers. Of course, you don't need a computer to make a flyer, but you'll find many other customer- and expense-tracking uses for your computer.

Truck farmer

What will I be doing?

Who would want to grow trucks? Actually, a truck farmer is a home-based business for those who want to select, cultivate, and sell vegetables, herbs, plants, and fruits to others for profit. It's a mini-farm that sells produce directly to consumers either at a roadside stand or at a local farmers' market. The term comes from the fact that the product is frequently sold out of the back of a pickup truck.

What will I need to start?

To be a successful truck farmer you need some land where you can grow things. You don't need 40 acres. In fact, you don't even need one acre. You can grow products in efficient greenhouses and get some of your income from selling for others. However, if you do have some tillable land, so much the better.

You'll also need some knowledge and experience growing and selling your products. Fortunately, there are many excellent books and courses on the topic available through Department of Agriculture Extension Service offices and through the Small Business Administration.

Who will my customers be?

Customers include individuals and restaurants. A produce stand by the highway, your booth in the local farmer's market, and delivery service to restaurants and flower shops are all opportunities to meet your customers. Meeting your customers can help you improve your product as well as benefit from the satisfaction of knowing that your hard work is appreciated.

How much should I charge?

It depends on what you're selling. Prices for your products will depend on local market conditions (what are rutabagas going for in your area these days?) and to whom you're selling (your asking price will vary depending on whether you're selling tomatoes to a vegetarian restaurant or at a roadside stand). Actually, you can learn how much to charge for your products by studying the marketplace and knowing your own costs to produce. A season of selling zucchini may tell you there's not enough profit and that raising sunflowers will bring you a better income. Whatever you grow, watch what people buy, how much they pay and how you can best use your "farm." Many truck farmers keep a thick spiral notebook of data, information, and ideas to make the comparison easier.

How much will I make?

So much depends on what you grow and the local market for that product. In general, a truck farm can expect $10,000 to $15,000 an acre depending on crop and number of seasons. Large greenhouses can bring in as much as $5,000 to $10,000 a year per greenhouse.

How can I get started?

The best way to start your truck farm is small. Plant one or two crops and learn as much as you can about growing and marketing them. Once you've learned what you can profitably grow and sell locally, you can increase your planting and harvest.

If you are depending on the local soil (rather than greenhouse soil), contact the local extension office for soil testing and suggestions. You may find that your soil is better for one type of crop over another. Also ask for advice on the best way to use your land.

Also visit the local farmers' market to see what's already being sold and what isn't. Talk with vendors. Many will be helpful even though you are a potential competitor.

How can I use computers to increase profits?

Truck farmers use computers in a variety of ways: to make pricing signs, list produce menus, track expenses, estimate future sales, research new plants, network with other truck farmers, and more. The first job for your computer is to track income and expenses.

Used-car inspection service

What will I be doing?

Deserved or not, used-car dealers have a bad reputation. Even those who buy used cars from the owner should be wary. If you know about cars and how to diagnose problems without expensive equipment, you can offer a valuable service to used-car buyers. You can start a used-car inspection service operated from your home.

A used-car inspection service, as you can guess, gets paid for inspecting and assessing the condition of used cars. Some services also offer pricing information based on official pricing books. Many of these services work out of their garage or from their own car.

What will I need to start?

First, you must know how cars run, what makes them not run, and how dishonest people can doctor a bad car to make it look and sound good. Fortunately, you don't have to be a 30-year mechanic to get this knowledge. You can read books and take courses from 30-year mechanics.

You'll need some basic mechanic's tools and test equipment. While a computer chip tester is useful on newer cars, it's surprising what you can learn about a car with a compression tester and a vacuum gauge.

Who will my customers be?

Your customers will be individuals wanting to buy a good used car at a fair price. They don't want to pay more than a car is worth because a mechanical problem was intentionally or unintentionally hidden from them. Using automotive pricing guides available at larger bookstores, you can also tell the potential buyer what the typical price should be for the car.

How much should I charge?

You will be paid for what you know. A used-car inspection service uses a shop rate of $30 to $70 an hour to set prices. The price quoted to the customer, however, will be based on the time it takes you for the typical job. An inspection that requires two hours of your time at $50 an hour is priced at $100. Another way of pricing is by a percentage of the value of the car. For example, you may price inspection of cars worth more than $2,000 in value at 5 percent of value. Seen as a small percentage, many customers will be less reluctant to hire you— even though your price will be the same or even higher.

How much will I make?

If you keep busy, your auto inspection service can net you an income of $30,000 a year or more. To keep busy when you're not inspecting cars, consider also doing minor repairs or even buying and reselling cars you inspect and guarantee. You can also sell your services to used-car lots, inspecting their vehicles and making recommendations on condition and pricing.

How can I get started?

You can start your auto inspection service based on knowledge and experience, but you will soon need advanced skill and even wisdom to make it grow. You will want a good reputation for honesty and fairness. You are offering a service based on trust.

Advertising will be important to you in trying to get the word out about your inspection service. Place an ad in your local newspaper and shopper car ad sections. Also make a brochure or flyer that you can distribute. It should include a description of your services, your pricing, your qualifications, and information on how to contact you. The more you help others the more you will be helping yourself.

How can I use computers to increase profits?

Your inspections will follow a specific structure listing automotive groups and components with a check-off and notes section for each. You can probably find a useful inspection form or you can use a computer to publish your own (with your company name and phone number on it). You can also print up your own business cards, brochures, and other promotional material. And you can use it to track customers and jobs. Handy!

Wallpaper service

What will I be doing?

One of my friends loves to wallpaper. She sees every painted wall as a challenge. She knows what papers look best in a room and, most important, how to apply them. If this describes you as well, consider offering a wallpaper service based from your home. You will select, prepare, install, trim, and remove printed wallpaper. Some wallpaper services contract directly to paint and paper stores while others work with remodeling contractors or directly with the public.

What will I need to start?

Hanging wallpaper, as anyone who has tried knows, is a skill. Doing it fast and well is a craft. To start a professional wallpaper service, you'll need to first develop your skills and crafts.

You will also need to know how to select the most appropriate wallpaper for a room, or advise your customer on how to do so. This requires some design training and experience. Many decorating books cover this topic adequately and can be purchased at larger bookstores or found in public libraries.

Equipment needed for hanging wallpaper is minimal. A ladder, a work surface (counter, card table, portable work bench), a tray, brushes, rollers, and seamers are all that's needed for most jobs. If you also remove wallpaper, buy removal tools such as a heat gun or steamer and putty knives. You will also need tools for preparing painted walls for wallpaper.

Who will my customers be?

Customers for a wallpaper service include individuals, companies, interior decorators, contractors, and retailers. Most services start with individuals and build the business and reputation, then move to contractors. Others who have friends and relatives in the contracting industry start there.

How much should I charge?

A wallpaper service establishes prices based on a rate of $30 to $70 an hour. Quoted prices are based on the square footage and complexity of the job. For example, a 120-square foot (10 x 12) room that requires three hours to prepare and paper at $40 an hour may be priced at $1 a square foot. If priced by the wall surface, the same room with 300 square feet of wall surface can be priced at 40 cents a square foot. The cost of wallpaper is added to this amount due to the wide variation in prices and quality.

How much will I make?

A full-time wallpaper service can earn a gross income of $750 to $1,500 a week. Deduct overhead expenses and your net income is $500 to $1,200 a week or about $25,000 to $60,000 a year. That's good money for a job that can also be fun. Of course, you must be very efficient at both installation and marketing, but it can be done.

How can I get started?

First, learn your trade. Develop your skills selecting and hanging wallpaper for yourself and others. If you do it for others at no charge, ask for a letter of recommendation and referrals when you're done.

As available, take classes from wallpaper manufacturers and decorating courses at a community college. Develop business cards and a flyer that tells more about your services, pricing, and references. Then distribute these marketing tools to individuals, interior decorators, paint and wallpaper stores, remodeling contractors, and others. Also include a small advertisement in the services section of your local newspaper.

Contact the Guild of Professional Paperhangers (513-222-9252).

The SIC code for wallpaper services is 1721-04.

How can I use computers to increase profits?

Wallpaper services can benefit from the Internet. You can not only keep up with the latest in decorating trends, but you can also research and order wallpaper materials from major national wholesalers who are as close as your computer. You can also manage and balance your checkbook.

Window replacement service

What will I be doing?

As long as there are rocks and baseballs, there will be windows that need replacing. Your job, should you decide to accept it, is to find such windows and make them as good as new. They are on houses, retail stores, as well as on cars and trucks. It's straightforward work:

a window replacement service removes damaged windows and/or frames and replaces them with new ones.

What will I need to start?

Window replacement is a skill that can be self-taught. There are many how-to videos at large building supply stores that show you how to cut and install glass panes, replace window units, and address other related skills. Other books and videos are available on replacing automotive glass.

Tools are basic: You'll need a hammer, screwdrivers, putty knives, an assortment of rubber suction cups (for moving and placing glass) and other tools depending on what you're replacing and where. If you're replacing a window 100 feet off the ground, for example, you will want some safety equipment.

You will also need a place to store glass sheets and a vehicle for transporting them. Car windshields and door glass can be installed in your garage so you won't have to go to their site as you will with a house or business.

Who will my customers be?

Customers for your window replacement service include individuals, retailers, malls, glass wholesalers, car owners, janitorial services, car dealers, little league baseball players, and others.

The best way to reach these potential customers is to keep your name in front of them all the time so they call you when a window suddenly needs replacement. Place an ad in the local telephone book and in service directories. In addition, produce a flyer or brochure on your services and give them to real estate agents, retailers, general contractors, car dealers, or anyone else who may call on you or refer others to you.

How much should I charge?

The typical rate for a home-based window replacement service is $35 to $70 an hour. However, most services quote prices by the size and quality of the glass and the difficulty of replacing it. Your glass wholesaler can help you establish competitive prices based on costs and required labor. Also, contact your local insurance agents to offer your services and to ask how they estimate the replacement price of a window.

How much will I make?

A full-time home-based window replacement service can earn an aggressive owner $35,000 to $50,000 a year in net income after paying overhead expenses. The more profitable services are those that work most efficiently and manage their costs well. They also know how to find more business when things are slow. (That doesn't mean going out and breaking windows!)

How can I get started?

If you have lots of experience replacing windows, you're nearly ready to start now. If not, find wholesale glass services in regional telephone books and talk with them about your plans. Start gathering the tools and equipment you'll need for your specialty. Talk with local insurance agents about breakage policies and deductibles. Many of your checks will be coming from them and they can send business your way.

Start advertising your services when you're ready and make sure that every customer you have is a walking advertisement for your skills and fairness.

The SIC code for window replacement services is 1751-05.

How can I use computers to increase profits?

Computers are useful to window replacement services and to other small home-based businesses. They track income, expenses, customers, inventory, supplies, suppliers, and more. They can also help you find professional associations and other window replacers who can teach you more about making money with your business.

Woodworker

What will I be doing?

If you enjoy making things with wood, consider turning your hobby into a full-time business as a woodworker. A woodworker designs, makes, finishes, and markets products made of wood and related materials. The finished products can include toys, birdhouses, carved figures, crafts, and furniture, depending on what one chooses to specialize in. Woodworkers can easily work and sell from home.

What will I need to start?

The key to success as a woodworker is craftsmanship. You must know your trade. If you have experience as a professional or hobby woodworker, you may already have the needed skills. If not, start now on getting them.

You'll also need tools. Which tools depends on what wood products you will be making. You may choose to carve wooden figures or make coffee tables or kitchen cabinets. The tools for each job are different.

You'll also need a source of materials at prices that offer you a profit. You may be able to establish a wholesale or contractor's account through a local lumber retailer or a national mail-order supplier, which can be found through trade magazines.

Who will my customers be?

Your customers will be decided by what you make and how you sell it. If you sell small wooden craft items at flea markets, your customers will be individuals that visit your booth. If you carve decoys, your customers may be individuals, retailers, or even wholesalers.

To reach your potential customers, learn as much about them as you can. What do they want? How much are they willing to pay? Where do they shop for these products? Who are your competitors? Become a customer for your product so you can learn how the customer buys.

How much should I charge?

The shop rate for woodworkers varies from $35 to $75 an hour. Newer woodworkers with few tools may earn less, especially during the first year of operation. Most products are priced by the estimated time and materials in them with an added factor of value. That is, if a product costs you $11 to produce and market but you know that people will buy it for $20, price it at $20.

For more specific information on pricing woodworking, read my book, *The Woodworker's Guide to Pricing Your Work* (Betterway Books), available at *www.MulliganPress.com*.

How much will I make?

Woodworking is a production business that requires 20 to 30 percent of your time for marketing. If you produce in quantity for wholesalers, your marketing time will be less than if you sell to individuals at flea markets.

Your overhead costs will range from 25 to 50 percent of your income depending on production costs. More expensive tools require more expense.

So your income as a full-time home woodworker can be $35,000 a year or more depending on both your woodworking skills, your marketing skills, and the products you specialize in.

How can I get started?

Learn your trade. Find woodworking products that you enjoy making and that people need or want to buy. Learn as much as you can about the marketing and pricing side of your trade as it can make the difference in your profitability.

The SIC code for woodworkers is 1751-06.

How can I use computers to increase profits?

Woodworking is a craft. To give you more time and money for your craft skills, use computers for the mundane job of recordkeeping. Use Quicken or Money software to handle your checkbook. Also use desktop publishing software and a digital camera to promote your skills and your business in brochures and on the Internet with your own Web site. And consider Computer-Aided Design, or CAD software, to develop woodworking projects.

5 Best Professional Businesses

Antique dealer

What will I be doing?

There are more than 38,000 antique dealers in the United States, with many of them operating from home. It's the perfect full-time business for those who love quality furniture. Antique dealers can be surrounded by the best of the past. And they can make a living doing what they enjoy. As a home-based antique dealer you will find, appraise, purchase, and sell antiques in your home, in a warehouse, or through a catalog.

What will I need to start?

If you've been an antique collector for very long you may already have some of the inventory you'll need to start your antique business. If not, you'll need to build some inventory to get started, and you can gather this by going to flea markets, estate sales, and garage sales. Find the source that works best and at the lowest cost for you. Or you may decide to only sell antiques on consignment from others. This can be an expensive business to get into, so learn as much as you can and plan each purchase well. If you live in a location where people can easily find your home, find out whether local zoning laws will let you set up a retail store in your home. If not, consider showing your antiques by appointment only or renting a retail location.

Who will my customers be?

Customers for your antique dealership include collectors and individuals who simply want to decorate their homes with antiques. More specifically, your customers will be people who appreciate the value of the types of antiques you sell. One Iowan who found himself in San Francisco discovered lots of customers for farmhouse antiques, but few sources. He made a trip back to Iowa, rented a truck, bought pieces at auctions and estate sales, and took them to the City by the Bay for resale. He knew what antiques his customers wanted and, as important, where to find these antiques.

How much should I charge?

Most of the antiques you sell will be priced at double your cost. You may find some well below value but you may also have to pay more for special items. If you sell on consignment, your fee will be about 25 percent of the selling price. You make less because you don't have to tie up your money by buying the piece. If you were to charge by the hour for your skills and overhead expenses, you would set an hourly fee of $40 to $80, paid either as a percentage of value or a flat fee.

How much will I make?

Income from selling antiques is variable depending on knowledge, skills, specialty, season, and many other factors. If your overhead expenses are about one-quarter of your income, your profit will be the remaining quarter, or 25 percent of sales. Sell $200,000 in antiques and your profit (before taxes) will be $50,000. Your overhead expenses will be less if you sell antiques from your home.

How can I get started?

If you are a knowledgeable antique expert with selling skills, you will be paid well. Learn as much as you can about your trade, your competitors, your customers, and how to help them buy. You'll also need inventory to get started, which you can gather by going to auctions, estate sales, flea markets or any other place where you might find antiques at reasonable prices. Also, join local and national associations that relate to your business. Through them you will learn how to profit from antiques.

The SIC for antique dealers is 5932-09.

How can I use computers to increase profits?

Antique dealers can benefit from modern technology. In fact, many of them buy, sell, trade, and price their antiques using the

Internet. One successful dealer of collectibles has sold hundreds of items to buyers around the world using eBay (*www.ebay.com*). Others use Amazon.com's auctions and zShops to sell from home (*www.amazon.com*). Log on and learn how.

Bookkeeping service

What will I be doing?

There are nearly 30,000 full-time bookkeeping services in the United States. Why are there so many? Because records must be kept as money changes hands. A retail store keeps books or records on sales by product, expenses by supplier, and wages by employee. These records are used to calculate profit for the owners and taxes for the governments.

If you have skills and training in bookkeeping you can put them to work keeping records for other businesses, thus building a business of your own. You can operate exclusively or partially out of your home depending on your needs and those of your customers.

What will I need to start?

To start a bookkeeping service you will need knowledge and experience in single- and double-entry bookkeeping. It will also be helpful if you know or have access to computer accounting systems. One successful operator furnished each client with a licensed copy of Quicken, a popular checking computer software program. Once a week she picked up the customer's files on diskette or by modem and developed reports for them.

Setting up a manual bookkeeping system requires only a few supplies such as journals and ledgers purchased at stationery stores. A computerized bookkeeping system will cost a few thousand dollars to establish.

Who will my customers be?

Your initial customers for a bookkeeping service will be other small businesses. You can work with those in a geographic area (shopping mall, suburb, business complex), a trade (gas stations, clothing stores, dentists), or a function (billing, disbursements). As you define your service you will be defining your customers and how to reach them. Promotional mailings or telephone calls to potential customers in an area or trade can help you build your customer base.

How much should I charge?

The hourly rate for bookkeeping services is typically $20 to $40. The lower rate will be for low-skill work such as making entries into a journal or ledger. The higher rate will be for advising clients on solving specific financial problems. You won't be working as a public accountant, but you can still offer useful advice on records. Most bookkeeping services price their work by the month with a small discount (5 to 10 percent) for annual contracts. If, for example, you specialize in keeping books for contractors, you can set your price by the estimated annual sales. You may also want to add a fee for each employee or subcontractor your client uses.

How much will I make?

Once established, much of your time will be billable to one client or another. Initially, you may spend up to 35 percent of your time marketing your business. Within a few months this marketing time should be down to 15 to 25 percent. You should always be looking for new customers to replace those that go out of business, hire a full-time bookkeeper, or otherwise drop your services. A bookkeeping service with 1,600 billable hours a year at $30 an hour will have gross sales of $48,000. Allowing 25 percent for overhead gives the owner a net income of $36,000 for the year.

How can I get started?

Before opening your home bookkeeping service you'll need sufficient training and experience to convince prospects to hire you. If you don't have extensive experience, get some by working for a bookkeeping service. Ethically, you should not go after their customers, but you can use what you've learned about the trade to build your own business. You may even find a service owner who wants to retire in a few years and is willing to sell to you.

For franchise information on a home-based bookkeeping business, contact General Business Services (800-583-9100).

Contact the American Institute of Professional Bookkeepers (800-622-0121).

The SIC code for a bookkeeping service is 8721-02.

How can I use computers to increase profits?

Here's a home business that really benefits from computers. Bookkeeping services with numerous clerks making ledger entries by hand (I used to work in one) are now replaced by one person, a computer, and bookkeeping software. In addition, you can consult for businesses that want to make their own entries then send you their "books" as an electronic file. In addition, you can offer tax service helping customers file not only annual income tax and quarterly reports but also payroll taxes.

Business consultant

What will I be doing?

As a business consultant you will help clients make informed decisions about subjects on which you have advanced knowledge and skills. Your expertise may be in managing professional offices, international marketing, computerized accounting, taxation, or other subjects. In each case, you will be paid for sharing your knowledge and your experience with others. You will be offering valuable advice to businesses.

What will I need to start?

To sell business solutions to others you must have successfully solved business problems yourself. This requires experience in business, along with good communication skills. You will also need plenty of resources to help you answer questions.

To start your business consulting service, make sure you have developed the knowledge and skills you need. This takes time and training. Then find ways of certifying your knowledge and experience so that prospects will trust you. For example, a business communications consultant can earn professional certification from the Business Marketing Association.

Who will my customers be?

Your customers will be business owners and managers who need solutions to problems they face. If your field is tax accounting, your customers will be business people with tax accounting problems. If you specialize in helping small businesses grow, your customers will be those who own small businesses that need to grow to survive. You get the picture.

How much should I charge?

Many business consultants charge $50 to $150 an hour for their services, plus expenses. Most customers will actually be charged by the project or on retainer. A project such as developing a new marketing campaign will have a fee that is based on the estimated number of hours to be spent on the project.

How much will I make?

Not all of your time as a business consultant will be billable to clients. In fact, most consultants can only bill clients for 50 to 75 percent of their time. That means 20 to 30 hours a week are billable. At $60 an hour, gross income is $1,200 to $1,800 a week. Deduct 20 to 40 percent for typical overhead expenses to calculate your net income.

Of course, it will take a few months or even years to develop a group of clients that can make your consulting service profitable. However, once built, this business can offer both financial and personal rewards.

How can I get started?

To sell advanced knowledge and skills, you must first have developed them. You must have extensive training and experience in your field. You will also need some way of measuring this experience for clients: a certain number of years in a prominent business position, professional certification, or some other measurable factor. Publishing articles or a book in your field can also help. In addition, make sure you join the primary associations in your trade. You will not only learn from membership, you will also develop resources and customers.

Here are two other resources: Association of Management Consulting Firms (212-697-9693) and Institute of Management Consultants (212-697-8262). In addition, consider ordering *The Upstart Guide to Owning and Managing a Consulting Service* by Dan Ramsey, available on the Internet *at www.MulliganPress.com.*

The SIC code for business consultants is 8742-01.

How can I use computers to increase profits?

The computer is your best tool for tracking prospects, clients, appointments, resources, business news, and for invoicing. You can even use presentation software to present your qualifications to prospects. Review the various types of computer software for business in Chapter 3. Then go online to search for resources that will help your consulting business grow.

Computer instructor

What will I be doing?

Computers are everywhere: businesses, homes, schools, and government. The computer revolution has grown so fast that many people are not up to speed on the technology and are afraid of computers because they don't understand them. If you *do*, maybe you can start a home-based computer instruction business.

Computer instructors teach users how to get the most from their computer. They don't have to be experts or programmers, but teachers. They need to know more about computers than their students and be able to transfer that knowledge.

What will I need to start?

The main requirement for starting your computer instruction business isn't a computer—you can rent classrooms with computers already in them. The primary ingredient is knowledge. You must understand how computers (hardware) and programs (software) work together to accomplish specific tasks. To gain this knowledge, read, practice, take a class, read some more, and practice some more.

For example, as many people were intimidated by the introduction of the Windows 95 operating system, one enterprising man set up a two-hour class that helped people become comfortable with it. He learned enough to teach the class by reading computer magazines, buying some books and videos on the subject, and spending some hours at the computer learning about the system. He then offered his class to businesses, through colleges, at high school computer labs, and any other place that used computers. He charged $20 a student and typically trained at least 10 students a day.

Who will my customers be?

Your customers for computer instruction will be both individuals and companies. You will earn more by instructing large groups because even though the per-student fee is smaller, the total income per hour is greater with groups. Computer instructors typically design classes around popular programs or applications, then produce a flyer to promote the classes. These fliers are then given to businesses and individuals. Every few weeks, the fliers are revised with new class dates. Most important, make sure your students are on your mailing list to receive information on advanced classes.

How much should I charge?

The hourly rate for computer instructors is typically $35 to $75 depending on the knowledge required and the number of students. That is, 10 students would be paying $3.50 to $7.50 an hour for your class.

Most computer instruction is priced by the class session or group of sessions. That is, a three-hour evening class may be priced at $15 per student. Other instructors offer a series of progressive classes with an easy-payment plan. Find out what your competitors charge and how you can offer more for less.

How much will I make?

About two-thirds of your time as a computer instructor will be spent instructing. The balance of your time will be used marketing your services, learning more about your subject, and setting up classes. A full-time instruction business may earn $800 to $1,000 a week. But some full-time computer instructors conduct classes, seminars, and individual instruction for businesses, making as much as $60,000 a year.

Depending on how you price your services and to whom you teach, your overhead expenses (classes, equipment, programs, office supplies, telephone, taxes) will range from 20 to 40 percent of your income.

How can I get started?

Training is available for those who want to be computer instructors. Of course, the training is available via computer. Many computer consultants get certification through Microsoft, Linux, Sun, or one of the other major system developers. Check their Web sites to learn more.

The SIC code for computer instructors is 8243-01.

How can I use computers to increase profits?

There are a variety of CD multimedia programs that help introduce the computer to people of all ages. You can use these programs as the core for classes or for individual instruction. For example, one such program helps older people with an interest in what's new learn more about computers. A computer instructor in Florida uses it as the core for her classes at retirement centers and nursing homes. Learning is a lifelong experience.

Computer maintenance service

What will I be doing?

Computers are wonders of electronics. Yet, like any other complex contraption, they sometimes fail. If you know how to fix them, you can earn a very good income doing so from your home.

A computer maintenance service, as you might expect, maintains and repairs computers at a customer's business site or at home. Related services are also offered by computer maintenance services. A remote backup service uses telephone lines and modems to make backup copies of information stored on customers' computers. A remote maintenance service diagnoses and repairs customers' software problems using telephone lines and modems.

What will I need to start?

To maintain and repair computers, you'll need to know how they work and what to do when they don't. Classes and books can help. You'll also need some tools: hardware tools and diagnostic tools. Hardware tools will help you open up a computer and replace components; diagnostic tools are software programs that can help you identify problems and their solutions. Another good idea is reading manuals on the subject. One such useful resource is *Upgrading and Repairing PCs* by Scott Mueller (Que), a 1,400-page book that offers information on nearly all aspects of computer maintenance and repair.

Who will my customers be?

Customers for your computer maintenance service can be individual computer owners as well as companies that don't have their own computer maintenance people. The more lucrative market is working with businesses that have more than one computer. They need and are more willing to pay for computer maintenance and repair.

One way to find customers for your service is to offer free diagnostic and troubleshooting services. There are software programs that will help you find problems on PCs. Offering this service to select prospects may turn them into customers as they learn how valuable you can be to them. Also, consider working on-call for computer stores to back up their repair service.

How much should I charge?

Computer maintenance typically earns an hourly rate of $35 to $75, depending on what's done and how efficiently it is completed. Most computer maintenance is priced by the task, such as backing up or copying system files priced by the megabyte (Mb) of storage. The hourly rate for computer repair is higher because the knowledge, skills, and tools are more valuable. A computer repair service will usually charge $50 to $100 an hour for repair. Because the time to repair a computer problem is difficult to estimate, most repair services charge by the hour.

How much will I make?

A full-time computer maintenance service can typically bill about 1,200 to 1,500 hours a year, once established. At $40 an hour, the gross income is $48,000 to $60,000 with about 60 to 75 percent of that going into the owner's pocket. It's one of the more lucrative home businesses available.

How can I get started?

First, learn your craft through books, classes, videos, and hands-on experience. Then gather your tools and start looking for customers. You may specialize in maintaining Windows NT, Novell, or LANtastic networks, or you may prefer to stick to maintaining PCs. If competition is high for general services, you may specialize in servicing printers or voice mail systems or other components. Find a need and fill it.

Contact the Independent Computer Consultants Association for more information (314-997-4633).

The SIC code for computer maintenance services is 7378-01.

How can I use computers to increase profits?

You already know how to use computers, but are you well versed on the various ways to make the computer your business partner? Many computer consultants set up a Web site for prospects and customers to help them understand more about their computer—and call *you* when they can't figure it out.

Computer programmer

What will I be doing?

This isn't a business for everyone. But if you have experience programming computers, you can become a freelance computer programmer working at home and making good money. A computer programmer writes instructions for computers in a language that the computer understands. Of course, computers really don't understand the way that humans do. Computers have "understanding" built into their hardware. A computer programmer simply applies the rules of computer understanding.

Most freelance computer programmers don't write system programs, the deepest level of instructions. Instead, they apply programs to specific applications. That is, they instruct accounting software how to keep records for a specific business or industry. So the programmer must know something about programming software as well as the field for which it is written.

What will I need to start?

As a computer programmer, you will be paid for applying what you know about software programs primarily for businesses. So the first step to your home-based business is to learn. Take classes on computers and programming through your local college or trade school. Learn about languages, operating systems, hardware architecture, and how they all work.

Most successful computer programmers specialize in one or more related fields. Remember: An expert is someone who knows more and more about less and less. So look to your own experience, training, background, and interests for ideas. Consider specializing in programming interactive games, accounting software, sales software, integrated systems, Windows NT systems, communications tools, or some other type of software that you find of particular interest.

Who will my customers be?

Many companies, government offices, institutions, and individuals need the services of a computer programmer. Most programmers find that businesses are their greatest customer. Some programmers specialize in one or two highly technical areas, such as programming industrial controllers. Others specialize in writing programming with a specific language, such as C++ or Visual Basic.

How much should I charge?

A freelance computer programmer will charge $40 to $150 per hour depending on skill level and competition. However, most programmers bid by the project and aim for efficiency. A few charge by what's called "lines of code" or the amount of programming code written.

How much will I make?

A freelance computer programmer can easily earn $35,000 to $80,000 a year or more—if he or she is efficient and the demand for services is high. Many computer programmers aim for at least 25 billable hours a week, with some averaging 50 hours or more. Of course, no one can maintain such a schedule for long and those who work long hours usually take some time off between jobs.

How can I get started?

To start your home-based computer programming business you'll first need to learn your trade by taking relevant classes and studying books. You'll also need to practice by developing one or more programs that you can then sell, or at least point to as an example of your work.

Also, getting a degree or certification will help customers trust you. Once established, word-of-mouth advertising will help your business grow as others learn what you can do and trust you to do it. Meet the people in your business, make friends and you can help each other. Your computer programming business will grow as you do.

How can I use computers to increase profits?

You know how to design programs and write and debug code. But do you know how to market your skills? There are many valuable tools for helping you do so. Programs like Act (available at most computer and office supply stores) help you track prospects and customers. QuickBooks and Microsoft Money help you manage the money you make.

Desktop publisher

What will I be doing?

Computers have revolutionized many businesses, including the publishing business. A growing field is that of computer-aided, or desktop, publishing. With the help of computers, thousands of people are starting part-time and full-time businesses in their homes to design and produce printed materials.

Computers are used to produce fliers, letterheads, brochures, business cards, slim jims (narrow brochures), envelopes, community newspapers, commercial newsletters, and many other creative products.

What will I need to start?

Desktop publishing requires skills and knowledge in a variety of areas, including design, computers, papers, colors business documents, as well as some writing or editing skills. For equipment, you'll need a computer, desktop publishing (DTP) software, a printer, and some supplies such as printer paper and toner cartridges. DTP software includes a page design program (Aldus PageMaker, Microsoft Publisher, Corel Ventura) and/or a word-processing program (Microsoft Word, Corel Word Perfect, Lotus Word Pro) and some drawing programs (Adobe Illustrator, Corel Draw, Paintbrush).

Who will my customers be?

Customers for your desktop publishing service include businesses, associations, and individuals. DTP services in smaller towns offer a wide variety of documents designed on computers while those in larger cities tend to specialize. One service may specialize in producing association newsletters while another offers small business startup sets that include letterhead, envelopes, business cards, and brochures or fliers for a set price.

How can you reach your customers? That, of course, depends on who they are. The best way is to develop your own creative business documents using your DTP skills and system, then mailing them to prospective customers. You may also want to place a small service ad in the business section of your local newspaper.

How much should I charge?

The hourly rate for desktop publishing service varies greatly with the value of the product you produce and your efficiency. Typically, the shop rate for DTP services is $35 to $75 per hour, but most jobs are priced by the product. You can calculate the amount of time required to produce your documents, or you can rely on DTP pricing books such as Robert Brenner's *Pricing Guide for Desktop Publishing Services* (Brenner Information Group).

How much will I make?

Most desktop publishing services require 30 to 50 percent of their time to market their services. This means that 50 to 70 percent of their time is billable. Overhead expenses (computer system and software, supplies, telephone, taxes) take 20 to 40 percent off the top of what you make. So a full-time desktop publisher working 40 hours a week at a shop rate of $45 an hour will gross about $1,080 and net $648 to $864 a week, depending on overhead.

How can I get started?

You can start your desktop publishing service today by learning more about the trade, the opportunities, and the costs. To help you get started, read my book, *Upstart Guide to Owning and Managing a Desktop Publishing Service* available from *www.MulliganPress.com*. Also consider joining the National Association of Desktop Publishers (508-887-7900).

The SIC code for desktop publishing services is 5734-03.

How can I use computers to increase profits?

Desktop publishing *requires* computers! But besides page layout and publishing, there are many other jobs your computer can do to earn its way. It can track customers, income, expenses, depreciation, checking accounts, and even schedule jobs. You can also put a beautiful Web site up on the Internet for the world to see your skills.

Editing/proofreading service

What will I be doing?

Are you frequently finding grammatical errors in books and magazines you read? Do you have a love for language that makes you look for ways of improving written communications? If so, consider establishing an editing or proofreading business in your home.

A proofreading service checks written materials for accuracy in grammar, spelling, punctuation, and style. An editing business helps others apply the rules of good communication to documents they write, focusing on content. Editing often requires some rewriting and reorganization of material. Many businesses offer both editing and proofreading services.

What will I need to start?

First, you must have a thorough knowledge of good written communication skills—including punctuation, grammar, and style. You may have a degree or simply an interest in English. You will, of course, have plenty of resources: a good dictionary, thesaurus, as well as style and grammar references. You will also need a knowledge of how documents are edited and corrections are marked using what are called "proofreader's marks." Most books on editing include these standard marks. Learn and practice using them.

You may use a computer for proofreading and editing, which will allow you to receive a document file from your client that you can transfer to your computer. Some word processors offer an editing mode that allows you to cross out and insert words as needed, documenting the changes you're suggesting.

Who will my customers be?

In some cases, your customers will be book, magazine publishers, or newsletter publishers. In others, your customers will be businesses preparing promotional materials, annual reports, or corporate brochures. Your customers may also include individuals who want your expertise on a resume or a manuscript they're submitting for publication.

Where can you find these customers? By listing your editorial services in *Literary Marketplace* (R.R. Bowker), in *Writer's Digest* magazine (at newsstands), or in other publications. You can also contact local desktop publishing services, writer's groups, newspapers, local magazines, and other communication companies to inform them of your services and fees.

How much should I charge?

The rate for editorial services varies depending on skills, complexity, and credentials. Many editing/proofreading services set rates of $25 to $60 an hour with lower rates for simple proofreading and higher rates for technical editing. Many jobs are quoted by the word or size of the project, calculated by estimating the time required and multiplying it by the hourly rate. Proofreaders may set fees of $6 per 1,000 words or $2 per manuscript page. Editing services will earn two to three times this fee, depending on time required to complete the job.

How much will I make?

At first, you'll spend at least half of your time building your skills and finding new business. Once established, 70 to 80 percent of your time will be billable. So you may be able to bill 28 to 32 hours in a 40-hour week. Your overhead costs for a home office, telephone, equipment, and resources will take 20 to 40 percent off the top. So an established editing/proofreading service can offer the owner an income of $25,000 to $60,000 a year.

How can I get started?

This job typically requires some credentials. You'll need some experience as an editor and perhaps a degree in English, communications, or journalism. However, you can build credentials by doing good work for your clients and building references.

The SIC code for editing services is 8999-13.

How can I use computers to increase profits?

Computers have revolutionized editing. Instead of red pencil marks on a double-spaced typewritten page, today's editing is typically done on computers. Programs allow multiple copies of a document to be edited by various people, then can incorporate all of the changes into a single document. Editing marks can be reviewed and either accepted or rejected by an editor. Editing services also benefit, of course, from using their computer to make the business more profitable with time-, customer-, and money-management software.

Event planner

What will I be doing?

Are you one of those people who love to plan events? Do you love all the arranging and preparing and detail that precedes a party or special occasion? Do you volunteer to set up meetings? If so, you may be able to turn your skills and interests into a profitable home business.

An event planner is hired to plan and coordinate meetings and other events for businesses, professionals, and individuals. Events that need planning can include annual board meetings, company picnics, alumni events, anniversary parties, and other get-togethers.

What will I need to start?

The first thing you need to start your event-planning business is organization skills. You must know how to manage a wide variety of elements needed for a successful event. You must be able to find and hire a caterer, make sure the podium and presentation elements are in place, find a meeting place, ensure there is adequate seating, promote the event, and much more. You may specialize in one or more types of events, but you must know how to efficiently organize any type of event.

Of course, you will need lots of resources: meeting places, presentation equipment, caterers, promoters, transportation, etc. These resources will make your job easier—or harder, depending on their abilities.

Who will my customers be?

Who will hire your event-planning services? Companies, associations, schools, and individuals are all potential clients. Companies who profit from your event will pay the best. For this reason, some event planners specialize in working with companies to plan sales meetings, board meetings, staff meetings, client meetings, and other events that can be profitable for the company—and for the planner.

How much should I charge?

Though you will price by the event, you will calculate the fee based on an hourly rate of $25 to $40 plus expenses. For example, if an annual stockholder's meeting takes 30 hours to plan and coordinate as well as $1,000 in expenses, your price for the event (at $30 an hour) is $1,900—call it $2,000. Or, if you are expecting about 50 attendees, you can price the event at $40 per attendee. That puts the event in terms your client can best understand.

How much will I make?

Event planning is a difficult business to grow quickly. It takes a lot of promotion and word-of-mouth advertising to build. But once established, it can be very profitable as clients hire you for annual events years in advance. Initially, only about half of your time will be billable to a client. Later, about 75 percent of your time will be billable with the balance used for marketing or administration. Expenses for your business are minimal beyond basic home office expenses and some advertising and brochures. Calculate overhead at 20 to 40 percent of sales. A new event planning service will struggle, but an established one can earn the owner $60,000 a year or more.

How can I get started?

Skills needed to plan and coordinate events take time to develop. If you don't already have them, start getting them now. Read books on organization, event planning, meeting coordination, and on business itself. You can pick up some of the skills—and some valuable references—by volunteering to coordinate an event for an employer, a friend's company, church, or other groups.

Contact Meeting Professionals International (214-712-7700) and the National Association of Professional Organizers (914-353-9270).

How can I use computers to increase profits?

Events require advanced organization skills—and tools. Computers can help you plan, organize, and schedule multiple events much easier than can be done on paper. Once you've joined a trade association, you'll get information about tools that other event managers use. Meantime, look at popular software tools for record-keeping, Web site design, and other business tasks.

Financial advisor

What will I be doing?

Are your credit cards paid off? Do you have a good start on your retirement fund? If so, you're ahead of most of us! Consider getting certified to become a financial advisor to help others get ahead. Guide clients in making informed decisions about the risks and rewards of specific financial investments and opportunities. You can offer a wide range of financial services, including estate planning, investing, and setting up trusts, either by working with businesses, small business owners, or with individuals.

What will I need to start?

There are more than 30,000 financial services and consultants in the United States., but there's always room for more good ones.

Many financial advisors have extensive training and experience working in the finance industry, but many others help us common folk manage our money better.

Depending on your knowledge, skills, and experience you may decide to consult businesses on pension plan investments or you may help home managers reconcile their bank statements. To give advice on financial matters, you must have success in doing so. Maybe you've built a successful business, done well in the stock market, or found other ways of increasing your net worth. Share your experience with others for profit.

Depending on the type of financial advice you offer, you may require licensing or bonding. It not only helps protect your clients from less-than-qualified advisors, it also helps protect *you* from fly-by-night competitors.

Who will my customers be?

Your customers will be defined by the type of financial advice you are most qualified to offer. If you have experience managing stock purchases, your customers will be those who typically invest in stocks and need some help. If you advise people of alternatives to bankruptcy, your customers are those who are now considering bankruptcy as their only option. Identify the best way to reach these customers: ads in the local newspaper or regional business papers, telephone marketing, association mailing lists, seminars, or other methods. Of course, as in most occupations, word-of-mouth referrals from satisfied customers are the best advertising of all.

How much should I charge?

Qualified financial advisors are paid well, typically $45 to $120 or more an hour. Some are paid by the hour. Others, particularly those who work with investments, work on a percentage of the assets managed in the "portfolio." A 2-percent commission on $1 million is $20,000. Many financial advisors justify their costs by showing clients how to increase return on investment by an amount greater than the commission. Other financial advisors establish a set fee for services. Many advisors start by setting fees at 10 to 20 percent less than their competition until business is established.

How much will I make?

As much as 50 percent of your time as a financial advisor will be spent on developing knowledge. You will be paid for this, of course, but not directly. Instead, your hourly rate will be higher to reflect this unbillable time that benefits all clients. Overhead expenses for your home office will be low, but subscriptions to financial news resources can be a major expense. Typical overhead expenses are 20 to 40 percent of gross income. A financial advisor can earn a net income of $50,000 or more annually once a client base has been established.

How can I get started?

First, decide what type of financial advice you are most qualified to offer. You can't make it clear to clients if it isn't clear to you. Second, find out what credentials, licenses, certificates, or other qualifications you will need to offer financial advice in your field. Get more than you need to illustrate that you are more qualified than your competitors. Third, get some customers. Good customers are the key to growth. If you have the qualifications, consider teaching one-time workshops on financial issues to attract customers.

The SIC code for financial services is 6282-03 and for financial consultants it's 6282-05.

How can I use computers to increase profits?

Computers have brought financial information gathering to a science. From your home, you can watch the stock markets of the world while you e-mail the latest data to your clients and prospects. You can also write and publish your own financial newsletters on paper and the Internet. And you can keep track of your clients' portfolios. All from home.

Freight broker

What will I be doing?

It's magic. Products made in far-off countries appear in retail stores even in the smallest communities. How do these products get from point A to point B? By ship, train and truck, of course. But there's another part of this process that many people aren't aware of: those who make sure that the products are transported efficiently and economically. These are the freight brokers. There are about 10,000 full-time freight brokers, consolidators, and forwarder services in the United States. They offer related services that require managing the contacts and the paperwork to move things from where they are to where they should be.

What will I need to start?

This isn't a business for everyone. It's best started by someone with experience in the transportation industry. One freight broker is a line-haul truck driver who wanted to get off the road. He now coordinates thousands of truckloads each year from his home office.

To start a freight brokerage, forwarding, or consolidating service, you'll need to know the industry and its players. Depending on your experience, you may decide to specialize in LTL (less than a truckload), containerized, or shipload freight services. You can learn about this business in books, but practical experience and contacts in the industry are vital.

Who will my customers be?

In most cases, you will work with manufacturers or wholesalers who want to move products to market. An equipment manufacturer may need to move large factory machinery to a buyer. A wholesaler may need a shipment of socks moved from Taiwan to the distribution center in Cincinnati. A company may need their exhibit equipment moved to a trade show in Dallas and back.

How will you reach these customers? Once identified, you can reach them through mailing lists, ads in trade publications, and through referrals.

How much should I charge?

The hourly rate for freight services ranges broad—$25 to $50 or more. In most cases, pricing of freight services is based on a percentage of the freight bill. These percentage fees vary as well, with higher percentages paid for smaller shipments. The fee also varies based on whether you are forwarding, consolidating, or brokering freight. In most cases, the marketplace will dictate your fee. If your calculations say it is profitable, go for it.

How much will I make?

Once your freight business is established, less than 20 percent of your time will be spent marketing your services. As your business grows, you may need even less time as repeat and referral business builds. Because you don't buy the freight you're shipping, your overhead costs are lower. A home office with telephone, computer, supplies, and taxes to pay will eat up 20 to 40 percent in overhead expenses.

How can I get started?

Again, this isn't everyone's home business. You will be paid in direct proportion to your knowledge of this industry and your ability to get things done quickly and economically. So, if your interest lies in freight brokering, learn your trade, develop organization and contact skills, work for someone else until you learn the business, then work for yourself.

The useful SIC codes are 4213-03 for a freight broker, 4731-02 for a freight consolidator, and 4731-04 for a freight forwarder.

How can I use computers to increase profits?

Besides using computers to gather shipping and freight information, you can use them to manage your contacts, your clients, and your cash. You can also promote your business with a Web site on the Internet to keep your customers informed and your prospects interested.

Graphic designer

What will I be doing?

If you enjoy designing and drawing, maybe you can join the nearly 19,000 professional graphic designers in the United States. You need skill and experience, but it is a rewarding business that can be operated from your home.

A graphic designer designs and produces brochures, advertisements, and other documents used in business. He or she turns ideas into compelling documents using colors, illustrations, and other graphics materials.

What will I need to start?

Graphic design is more than just drawing. It requires artistic skills, advanced training in graphic design and, in today's world, familiarity with computers. Most larger community colleges offer courses in graphic design and related topics if you need them. The best way to start is to get some experience in the field working for a graphic design house, an advertising agency, or any other professional office where you can build your skills and your reputation.

For many years, graphic design was done with pen and paper. Today's graphic designers frequently use computers. In fact, there are many excellent software programs that will help you design good-looking documents with minimal effort. So you may need a computer to start your graphic design business.

Of course, your best tool in starting your business is samples. Most graphic designers spend a lot of time and energy in designing and producing their own business promotion literature.

Who will my customers be?

A great deal of your graphic design work will be for companies, specifically businesses who are marketing to others. Your job is to help them present their products or services in the best possible light. A secondary market will be designing graphic products for advertising agencies that work for businesses.

How can you find customers? One enterprising graphic designer collects brochures and ads that she feels she could improve, then makes an appointment with the company to offer suggestions at no cost. Of course, she is careful how she presents her ideas so as not to offend. This method has multiplied her graphic design business threefold in the first year.

How much should I charge?

Most graphic designers charge $40 to $75 an hour, but you should price by the product or by the percentage of value. For example, a standard brochure may require three hours of time. At $50 an hour, the designer can quote a price of $150 for designing a brochure. Some graphic designers price as a percentage of the value of the resulting document. For example, a 24-page catalog with a production and printing cost of $32,000 could be designed at 10 to 15 percent of that cost, or $3,200 to $4,800. Or the designer could quote a rate of $135 to $200 per catalog page.

You can initially price your services at about 10 percent less than competitors with comparable qualifications. Once your business is built you can begin increasing your rates until you have the best balance of business and profits.

How much will I make?

Once established, you should be able to bill for 70 to 80 percent of your time—28 to 30 hours a week. With an estimated overhead cost for your home office of 20 to 40 percent of sales, you can earn a net income of $30,000 to $80,000 a year before taxes.

How can I get started?

There is an abundance of graphic designers with few credentials, so your business must be built on your unique skills to be competitive. Start by developing these skills as you simultaneously look for the best way to market them. It will help if you have professional credentials and lots of experience. And remember, one of your greatest sales tools is your own business graphics. Make sure your business cards, stationery, brochures, and other materials reflect your knowledge and skills.

The SIC code for graphic designers is 7336-03.

How can I use computers to increase profits?

Graphic designers use computers profitably in many ways. Of course they do use computers to design and produce their graphic products. But they also use computers to promote their skills over the Internet, track customers, market to prospects, as well as develop portfolios and presentations. You can even send your work to clients electronically using your computer.

Import/export service

What will I be doing?

Importers and exporters have a vital job in our world's economy—they trade products and services internationally. They profitably move products from the maker to the user. Without them, we would not have many of the things we enjoy each day—from cars to calculators. And, best of all, because of modern communication technology, importers and exporters can work anywhere—including from home.

What will I need to start?

To join the more than 12,000 import agents and nearly 17,000 export agents in the United States, you must know the import/export business, foreign markets, products and services, business, and international trade and money. So first learn as much as you can about international trade. Fortunately, there are many excellent books on the subject in most larger libraries and bookstores. But you'll need more. You'll need contacts in the business community, permits, tariff books, and many other resources.

Who will my customers be?

Your customers will be manufacturers and wholesalers in the United States and other countries. If you are importing products into the United States, you will contact manufacturers in other countries, learn about their products, then find markets here for those products. If you export, you'll find U.S. manufacturers and wholesalers who want to expand their sales through international marketing.

The Small Business Administration office in your region (see area telephone books) can help you find out about international trading resources and opportunities. They can even help you with the international banking aspects of this business, as will the U.S. Department of Commerce.

How much should I charge?

There is no hourly rate for import or export services. These services typically use what is called "value-added" to profit. In other words, for locating international buyers and sellers, they are paid either a percentage or a profit from the sales. For example, an importer of computer components may only earn a fee of 1 percent, but that's 1 percent of a sum that could easily be in the millions of dollars. An exporter of heavy equipment, on the other hand, may make a fee of 5 to 10 percent, but on a sale that may be substantially lower in value than the computer components.

How much will I make?

As a successful import or export agent you can earn a net income of $35,000 to $60,000 or more. Much depends on what products or services you're trading, competition in the market, the value of your resources and contacts, and some plain old-fashioned luck.

How can I get started?

If you're interested in import or export trade, start reading up now. Read books on the topic, newspapers (especially the international business stories), and magazine articles. At first, focus on any areas in which you have knowledge such as a specific type of product, a certain part of the world, a specific language, or any other advantage you have.

The SIC code for importers is 5099-05; for exporters it's 5099-01.

How can I use computers to increase profits?

Import and export services require that you keep up on economic and political changes in the world. Fortunately, you can use a computer to help you. In addition to the many news sources online (CNN, Bloomberg, NY Times), there are a variety of resources specific to importing and exporting products. And, of course, you can keep in touch with suppliers in Indonesia and buyers in Wales using the power of your computer and the new Electronic Age.

Income tax preparation service

What will I be doing?

There are more than 75,000 full-time income tax preparation services in the United States. What does an income tax preparation service do? It gathers and prepares income tax information and advises clients on how to legally pay the least taxes. All tax services handle federal income taxes and, if required, state income taxes. They help businesses calculate quarterly estimated tax payments. They make recommendations on reducing tax obligations.

What will I need to start?

Most people who start an income tax preparation business have degrees in accounting and some work experience in the area of tax preparation. To advise and prepare tax returns, you must understand the IRS tax codes and take classes and read appropriate publications to *continually* update your knowledge. There are community college and adult education classes on income tax preparation available in most areas. Correspondence courses are also available. Because the code is so complex, most tax preparers develop their expertise in one or two areas of it. Some help individuals prepare the annual *Form 1040*. Others specialize in helping small businesses with the *Schedule C* part of the *1040*. Others work with investors who have tax preparation questions.

An important factor to take into consideration is that, to a great extent, this is seasonal work. Even though many tax documents need to be prepared quarterly and monthly, the tax preparer's high season is from January 1st to April 15th.

Who will my customers be?

Your customers will be individuals, small businesses, and organizations such as nonprofits and trade associations. You'll find them by advertising your services and making it easy for them to find you. Most individuals start thinking about taxes in February when the last of their *W2s* arrive in the mail. Small businesses think of taxes most in December and January, but also have to think about them quarterly. Large businesses think about them every day.

How much should I charge?

The hourly rate for income tax preparation services varies with the level of knowledge and skill offered. The typical range is $35 to $80 an hour. However, standardized tasks can be priced by the task. For example, preparing *1040* forms for a married couple filing jointly with less that $100,000 in income and standardized deductions may typically take you three hours to prepare and file. If so, at an hourly rate of $60, you could price this service at $180.

To help you determine pricing, find out what other income tax preparers in your area are getting for their services.

How much will I make?

Most people don't need to be sold on the need for income tax preparation services. Basic advertising and word-of-mouth advertising will bring customers to you at tax time—though you may want to advertise more the rest of the year to bring in more income. The point is that advertising costs won't eat up much of your income. However, tools such as books and computer software will. Your overhead expenses will range from 20 to 45 percent depending on who your customers are and whether you have the latest in computer systems. An income tax preparer can make $35,000 to $65,000 a year working from home, depending on what related services are offered.

How can I get started?

If you have a background in accounting but don't have training or experience in income tax preparation, take some classes and read some books. Read lots of books. Keep current on tax law changes. As with other businesses, you will be paid according to what you know.

Contact the National Association of Tax Practitioners (414-749-1040; *www.natptax.com*) for more information.

The SIC code for income tax preparation services is 7921-01.

How can I use computers to increase profits?

Today's tax preparers can submit their clients' taxes electronically for faster returns. In addition, IRS forms and instructions can be downloaded 24 hours a day from *www.irs.gov*. The IRS Web site can also give you tax tips and other tools for helping your clients. In addition, there are powerful tax preparation software programs available that can streamline the tax preparation process. Some programs allow you to keep data for numerous clients.

Information broker

What will I be doing?

In today's economy, information is one of the most valuable commodities. With accurate information you can make money on the stock market, in real estate, or you can enhance nearly any business. Do you love to gather information? Are you a researcher by heart? If so, consider a home business as an information broker. What do information brokers do? They find and furnish valuable, hard-to-find information for specific customers.

What will I need to start?

To start an information brokerage service in your home, you'll first need to know how to find valuable information. Most information brokers use computers to search electronic databases, so you will need access to a computer as well as an understanding of how to use it. Depending on the type of research you will be doing, you may need membership in online database services. Some researchers start their business ventures using public resources such as libraries and the computers at larger libraries.

Who will my customers be?

Most information brokers specialize in one or more fields. If your background is in rocket science, you'll know how to find answers to specific questions about propulsion systems. If you have business experience, consider offering valuable information to business questions.

As an example, the owner of a successful pizza parlor was considering franchising her operation. An information broker helped her analyze other pizza franchises, discover the best location for a second store, and identify attorneys who could help her with the legal aspects of franchising.

How much should I charge?

The hourly rate for information brokers ranges from $45 to $120. The difference is in the value of the information to your customer. If your customer has a curiosity about Continental Mark II automobiles, for example, he or she probably won't pay much for the information. But if a business needs information that will help it launch a new million-dollar product line, your services will be very valuable.

Some information brokers charge by the hour, others price by the project (based on estimated time) or by a percentage of the value of the information. To do so, a business information broker may ask a client what the resulting information will be worth to the buyer, then price it accordingly.

How much will I make?

Because many people don't even know how an information broker can help them, you will spend extra time educating prospects. In fact, 20 to 30 percent of your time will be needed for marketing and even more as you start up your business. Overhead expenses range from 20 to 50 percent depending on whether you include research costs (online charges, books, photocopies) in your hourly rate or add them separately to the bill. Some customers want itemized expenses while others prefer a single price. Remember, though, that if you tell your customers the source of your information, they may decide to go directly to it next time.

A full-time information broker can net $30,000 to $75,000 a year working 40 hours a week. Some information brokers do their research evenings and weekends when online databases are less expensive to access. These databases will cost $20 to $150 an hour during the business day.

How can I get started?

Start learning how to research. Decide whether you will research online or the old-fashioned way. Decide who your customers will be and what they will want to know. Then find out where you can get the information for them with the least effort and expense. Finally, start contacting prospective customers to let them know about your services.

If you're uncomfortable with charging high hourly rates, offer discounted rates for the first few months of your business. By then your skills will be developed and your customers will see the value of your service. If you do offer a discount, trade it for a letter of recommendation.

For more information call 212-779-1855 for the Association of Independent Information Professionals.

How can I use computers to increase profits?

Information is your product —and computers are your tools. The Information Age was born with the computer. You cannot run a competitive information brokerage today without a computer. So learn to use your computer for information mining on the Internet, online databases, online libraries, and on CD-ROMs. Take classes, if needed, on using the Internet. Use the many search engines (Yahoo.com, Looksmart.com, Northernlight.com, etc.) to dig up information for your clients and for yourself.

Interior-decorating service

What will I be doing?

If you have skills or an interest in interior decorating, you may want to consider operating a decorating service from your home. Decorate what? You can design and decorate homes, offices, retail stores, or other places where people live and work. And you can be paid well for doing what you enjoy.

There are more than 30,000 full-time interior-decorating services in the United States, so there's lots of competition. But a decorator that offers service and value to a defined group of customers can find success.

What will I need to start?

Of course, to start an interior-decorating service you must have both knowledge and experience in the field. That's what you're selling. The more you know, the more you can help—and the more you can make. So learn your trade with courses, books, and practical experience as a decorator working for someone else.

Who will my customers be?

Your customers for interior-decorating services will be individuals, furniture stores, retail businesses, business offices, and even churches. Specialize in serving the decorating needs of a specific group of customers where your skills and interests are strongest.

Once you've defined who your customers are, finding them will be easier. For example, if you prefer to decorate the homes of the rich and famous, start contacting the rich and famous in your area. If there aren't many, you may have to move to where they are, or you may need to expand to serve those who want to *appear* rich and famous.

How much should I charge?

Your hourly rate for an interior-decorating service will be $35 to $75. Most decorators stay on the lower end of this range for many years until they have too much business, then they increase rates until the amount of work is just about right.

Interior-decorating services often help customers establish a budget, then price services as a percentage of the budget. For example, an office complex that will spend $20,000 on redecorating may get a bill of 10 percent—or $2,000 from the decorator. Other decorators charge the customer less, but earn a percentage on sales from suppliers where the furnishings are purchased.

How much will I make?

You'll spend 20 to 30 percent of your time seeking new business. That leaves 70 to 80 percent of your time billable—once your business is off the ground. If you are only advising customers, not buying any of the merchandise yourself, your overhead costs (including taxes) will range between 20 to 40 percent. Advertising will take up more of your budget for the first year or two, then that expense will taper off as your name is better known.

How can I get started? .

Join trade associations that give you credentials. Find a way of showing why your services are better than those of your competitors. Get letters of recommendation from any of your customers who are well known and respected in your community. Pick a good business name, get your business licenses and permits, design a quality brochure, and start promoting yourself in local news media. You'll soon have a profitable business doing what you love.

The SIC code for interior-decorating services is 7389-02.

How can I use computers to increase profits?

Interior decorators use computers to keep up on the latest styles, products, services, and ideas. They also use computers to track jobs, find prospects, order materials, and even to design. Make sure you're comfortable with using a computer in your interior decorating business—because your competitors probably are.

Local tour service

What will I be doing?

Is your town special? Are there things of interest that visitors to your town or city want to see? Can you show them the sites? A local tour service does just that: It researches, designs, plans, promotes, and operates tours of an area. It may focus on a famous historic district or nightclub circuit, or it can offer guided tours of natural scenery. It offers a view of your area that visitors can take home with them without stuffing their luggage. A Reno, Nevada, tour operator offered a special tour for nongamblers that focused on the historical aspects of the town.

What will I need to start?

No matter where you live, there's probably a site or two of interest in your town or area. If you have a good familiarity with the sites that would appeal to visitors, you're well on your way to gaining the expertise needed to conduct local tours. If the sites are historical in nature, read up about the buildings, neighborhoods, and people. Check the local library as well as old newspaper articles. If your area has some beautiful natural terrain, familiarize yourself with it by walking it, perhaps with someone from an area nature center. Become an expert on your product—your town.

In addition to a thorough knowledge of your community, you will find presentation and creative skills to be an advantage. You must put together a "tour package" that will be interesting and entertaining to visitors. You don't necessarily need a vehicle for your tour service. You can hire a private bus service to provide transportation, offer walking or bicycle tours, or simply hire yourself out to guide other companies' tours.

In one mid-sized Midwestern city, two women who had given some tours to visitors of their synagogue became familiar with the Jewish history of their city. They included on their historical tour old buildings, neighborhoods, and businesses tied to the Jewish community, then later expanded to highlight other ethnic neighborhoods. They ultimately developed a fascinating historical tour of different ethnic communities in the city.

Who will my customers be?

Your ultimate customers will be those who travel to or through your area. They may come for business or pleasure. You may reach them individually, through hotels, or through local businesses that may bring in clients or business associates to the city. Your customers will also be tour operators and travel agents who book destinations. Sell them on selling their customers.

A third group of customers will be the people who already live in your area—the locals. They may want to know more about the area or suggest places that visitors can see while in town. Even school groups may be interested in your historic tour of the city or a nature walk through a local state park.

How much should I charge?

The price of your local tour service depends on many factors, the greatest being how well you can promote your business. A low-key tour service may earn just $25 an hour while one that is efficiently managed and marketed can bring the operator $60 an hour or more.

Tours are typically priced by the number of customers or a percentage of the total package. For example, a two-hour tour of local sites for a charter bus company may earn you 50 percent of the ticket price. The bus company gets the other half. If there are other stops on the tour you may have to split the take with them. Of course, you can handle the whole package, hiring the bus or other transportation, selling tickets, and finding other tour sites.

How much will I make?

If you operate a small, one-person local tour service from your home, overhead expenses will be less than one-third of your income. Spending a quarter of your time marketing, you may be able to build a tour service that not only offers you an income of $30,000 a year or more, but also employs part-time tour guides so you can spend your time finding more business.

How can I get started?

Start in your own neighborhood. Look for locations, events, sites, and other interesting points that you can promote into one or more tours.

Next, look for potential customers who may be interested in visiting these sites. Are there local travel agents who will promote your service? Are there fraternal organizations, professional groups, hobbyists, educators, or others who would enjoy your tours?

Finally, set a fair price and start marketing your local tour service. Once you've developed some experience, you can make changes in your tours and pricing to ensure profitability while discouraging competition.

Read *Upstart Guide to Owning and Managing a Travel Service* (Upstart Publishing) by Dan Ramsey available at the Web site *www.MulliganPress.com.*

Contact the National Tour Association (800-682-8886) for more information.

The SIC code for tour operators is 4752-01.

How can I use computers to increase profits?

Local tour operators typically use computers to promote their services to the world. Imagine: Some traveler living in Solengen, Germany, or Seoul, Korea, can pop on the Internet and see your Web site offering specifics on your local tours any time of the day or night. Register a URL (see Chapter 3), build a Web site, and start telling the world why they should visit your area.

Magazine writer

What will I be doing?

A magazine writer researches, develops, and sells articles to magazines and newsletters. Some writers specialize in a field, such as aviation or consumer finance, while others prefer to be generalists writing about a variety of topics. A typical day for a freelance magazine writer will include researching a topic, writing query letters, making calls to editors and, of course, writing. A magazine writer is paid for both creativity and craft.

What will I need to start?

Of course, to get paid well for writing you must know how to write well. There are excellent books, classes, seminars, and correspondence schools that will help you learn and apply the craft of writing.

There was a day not long ago when all the tools you needed to be a writer were a pen and paper. Today you need a computer to access online research sources, to write using a word processor, and even to deliver your manuscript electronically.

Who will my customers be?

Customers for your articles will be magazine and newsletter publishers. Which ones? That depends on what you're writing about. The annual edition of *Writer's Market* (Writer's Digest Books) is an important tool in finding buyers for your articles. Your local newsstand is another valuable resource as the editor's name and address for submissions is usually found in the front of the publication.

Once you have identified which publications would be good sources for your articles, write or call to request editorial guidelines and schedules. This information will help you determine how and when to submit article proposals—or queries.

You will market your ideas in what's called a query letter—a letter to the editor describing your proposed article and why it will be useful to the magazine's readers.

How much should I charge?

Magazine article writers establish an hourly or daily rate that helps them calculate profitability. The typical rate is $25 to $50 an hour. However, most magazines pay by number of words. An editor might offer you $450 for an 1,800-word article, based on 25 cents per word. If you figure it will take you nine hours to research and write the article, you will have earned $50 an hour. If it takes you more than 30 hours to write the article, it may not be such a lucrative opportunity.

You will be paid separately for photographs and drawings, if you provide them. You may also be able to sell reprint rights to another publication or keep them for a book you're writing, but don't count on these opportunities until you've established your writing business.

How much will I make?

You'll spend 20 to 30 percent of your working time trying to sell your work. Some writers set aside a full workday each week for marketing while others develop and market article ideas a couple of hours each day. Overhead expenses are lower than many businesses because you don't need inventory or expensive supplies. Typical overhead expenses are 15 to 25 percent of gross income. As a rule of thumb, professional writers get to keep about half of the money that comes in the mailbox. The other half pays for overhead, taxes and a couple of bucks toward retirement. As a magazine writer you can earn $30,000 to $60,000 a year once you are established and become recognized as an expert in your field.

How can I get started?

Writing is a craft that can be learned through classes, books, and lots of practice.

Here's a valuable secret about writing: writers really don't write. Instead, they pre-write, then write, then rewrite. Pre-writing involves researching and organizing facts on a topic, writing is putting them on paper, and rewriting is correcting and improving the writing until it reads effortlessly.

Identify publications you would like to write for and send away for editorial schedules and writer's guidelines—then spend time developing queries to send off. Or find a small magazine that you enjoy, read it over carefully a few times trying to define who the magazine's reader is, then write an article of interest to that reader and submit it to the magazine. Start small and learn your craft. (My first sale was to *Numismatic Scrapbook Magazine* in 1962!)

How can I use computers to increase profits?

Besides being a great tool for writers, the computer is also a valuable tool for magazines. Not only do many magazines publish condensed versions on the Internet, many also consider magazine proposals and accept articles submitted via e-mail. Learn more about electronic submissions in the latest annual version of *Writer's Market* available in bookstores. The electronic edition includes a CD-ROM to make market searching easier.

Mail-order sales

What will I be doing?

We've all seen the ads in the back of magazines: "How to Make a Million Dollars in Mail Order! Learn how: $10." In that case, the answer is: Get 100,000 people to send you $10 each! But the real answer is: Sell things people need and want by mail.

Mail order isn't really a business. It's a way of *doing* business. It uses the mail service or package delivery services to market and distribute products and services. In most cases, these are products that may not be available locally. Typically, you'll need to have an inventory (or access to inventory) of a product, whether it's your own line of cookies—or eyebrow tweezers you can get from a cheap source.

What will I need to start?

To sell by mail, you need a product or service that others need and are willing to buy and receive by mail. It must be a product or service that can be easily delivered by mail. Elephants-by-Mail is a poor business idea. Elephant-Books-by-Mail is better. You will need knowledge of shipping methods and costs. Some products are easier to ship than others. Some must be shipped economically while others need to get to the customer fast. What shipping services you use depends on the customer's needs and willingness to pay.

Your mail order business depends on your knowledge of marketing—how to find and keep customers. The more you know about reaching your customers, the less you will waste on unneeded advertising in the wrong outlets, and the more efficiently you can target your customers.

Who will my customers be?

Who will buy from you sight unseen? Those who have developed trust in mail order products and who need a product they can't find otherwise. You may be the exclusive manufacturer of a product for fishermen. You may offer 100-percent satisfaction guaranteed on everything you sell. You may offer free overnight delivery. You may only sell to the affluent.

A Texas tamale maker dramatically expanded business by offering tamales by mail. I'm not kidding. The tamales, individually wrapped and frozen, are shipped via overnight freight to customers around the world. A brochure sells the product, a toll-free telephone number is used for ordering by credit card. FedEx does the rest.

Sure, you can buy tamales at the local supermarket, but not *these* tamales!

To be successful in the mail order business you need to identify the customer and market niches for your product and reach them through the proper advertising and marketing. One way to do this is by purchasing mailing lists from other direct marketers.

How much should I charge?

In many cases, mail-order services have an hourly rate of $30 to $75. Most, however, prefer to use a markup or multiplier to cover the extra expenses of advertising and shipping. A common multiplier is three. That is, a product that wholesales for $10 is sold by mail for $30—or $29.95. Some mail-order businesses use lower or higher multipliers, but this one is the most popular.

How much will I make?

An efficient mail-order service can bring the owner an income of $30,000 to $50,000 a year in net income depending on what is offered and how efficiently it is sold. Mail-order businesses typically have a forgotten advantage over retail stores: "S & H" (shipping and handling charges). The mail-order price is $29.95 plus $4.95 for shipping and handling, which translates into savings for you because the customer is directly paying one of your major expenses—shipping and handling.

How can I get started?

First, identify your potential customers, learn about their needs, find products that fulfill those needs, and learn to price and distribute those products efficiently. Also, read my book, *Upstart Guide to Owning and Managing a Mail Order Business* (Upstart Publishing), which includes hundreds of mail-order business ideas as well as specific information on pricing and marketing. If you can't find it in your local bookstore, you can buy it online at *www.MulliganPress.*com.

How can I use computers to increase profits?

Mail-order businesses are using the Internet to reach a new and broader audience. Nearly all of the mail-order catalog merchants of yesterday (Sears, Spiegel, L.L. Bean, etc.) now have huge online catalogs. So can you. Well, maybe not *huge*, but profitable. Besides standard Web site design software, you will need programs that access your product database as well as online payment services through a "secure server." Start your education today by seeing how other mail-order businesses have profited online.

Newsletter publisher

What will I be doing?

Newsletters inform and promote to a variety of readerships. Hospitals use newsletters to promote their services with publicity written as news stories. Companies promote their products and services to customers and prospects with newsletters. Associations promote themselves and their members with newsletters. A newsletter publisher designs, researches, writes, and produces newsletters for business clients for distribution to their customers. Publishing a newsletter requires writing, editing, producing, and printing news documents for a target group.

What will I need to start?

As a newsletter publisher, you may design and write the newsletter but leave production to a desktop publishing service. If you do your own production, you'll need a computer, a printer, and desktop publishing software. You'll also need some training or experience using these tools.

To publish newsletters for others, you'll need writing, printing, and promotional skills. Many of these skills can be developed as an employee of a newsletter service or in the promotions department of a large company.

Who will my customers be?

Most newsletters are published by and on behalf of business and business groups. Those done for smaller charities and individuals are produced by volunteers. So you can volunteer to produce a newsletter to develop the skills you need to offer a newsletter publishing service for money.

How much should I charge?

The hourly rate for newsletter publishing is $30 to $70, but most are priced by the issue or the page. For example, a newsletter publisher may research, write, produce, and mail company newsletters for $500 to $1,000 per published page (plus printing and postage costs). That means the publisher is estimating 15 to 30 hours a published page at about $35 an hour.

How much will I make?

Marketing will take up 20 to 30 percent of your time once your business is established. Overhead expenses will take 30 to 40 percent of what you make for computer software and supplies, office expenses, taxes, and other necessities. A successful newsletter publisher can earn a net income of $25,000 to $40,000 a year or more.

How can I get started?

If you don't have a lot of experience, volunteer to produce newsletters for one or two of your favorite charities or an organization you belong to. They will pay costs while you donate your labor. If you do this, make sure you specify how long you are willing to make this donation. Depending on the group's budget, you may be able to ask a small fee for future work.

Contact the Newsletter Publishers Association (800-356-9302).

The SIC code for newsletter publishers is 2721-04.

How can I use computers to increase profits?

Many professional newsletters are now delivered exclusively online. There are no printed versions. Why? Because the information they deliver is outdated by the time that is published using traditional means. Instead, online newsletters can immediately deliver fresh information via e-mail and Internet Web sites. All that's needed are common e-mail programs such as Microsoft Internet Explorer and Netscape Navigator. Both also allow you to compose Web pages in HTML (HyperText Markup Language) and deliver them to your Web site.

Personal image consultant

What will I be doing?

Everybody needs some good advice. If people describe you as knowledgeable and helpful, consider becoming a paid personal image consultant. As a personal image consultant you will offer clients advice on wardrobe planning and personal shopping and provide corporate clients with workshops and seminars on professional etiquette. Individuals who want to feel better about themselves may also seek your services.

What will I need to start?

You will be selling both knowledge and wisdom on a specific personal subject. You may be selling your ability to select clothing or help clients make good choices. You must also be personable. Friendly advice sells better than unfriendly information. So you'll need patience, diplomacy, and some human psychology.

Who will my customers be?

Most of your customers, understandably, will be individuals. You will be offering them advice to help them present a better image—whether professionally or personally. Your customers will be those who don't feel their image is what they want it to be. Or your customers may be corporations who want to help employees project professional images.

You can also offer your personal image consulting services to groups through seminars and classes that you design or that are established by local colleges.

How much should I charge?

Personal image consultants earn an hourly rate of $30 to $70 or more. Well-known personal consultants who have written popular books on their topics earn much more. Most personal image consultants price their services by the value of the expected results. That is, a personal image consultant who helps enhance the image of corporate executives will charge more than for a similar service to new college graduates.

How much will I make?

Many people will be reluctant to use your services unless they have heard good things about you. Thus, it will require some time to develop your own image. Once established, you'll probably spend 20 to 30 percent of your time marketing your services.

Fortunately, overhead expenses for personal consultants are usually low. Advertising will be your largest expenditure. Otherwise, it's telephone, office supplies, and taxes. Expect 20 to 40 percent in overhead expenses. Selling 1,500 hours of your time each year at $40 an hour with 25 percent overhead expenses offers you a net income of $45,000 for the year.

How can I get started?

First, become an expert in your area. If you consult on clothing or makeup, make sure you know as much as you can about these topics. Read, study, learn, try, ask.

Second, let others know you're an expert. If you have successfully consulted people, ask for a letter of recommendation or other references. Write an article about your topic for a newspaper or magazine and, if published, get copies out to potential customers. Check area telephone books for other personal image consultants and learn from them.

Contact the Association of Image Consultants (800-383-8831).

The SIC code for personal image consultants is 8742-03.

How can I use computers to increase profits?

Believe it or not, computers can help personal image consultants make more money. Computer programs are now available that make makeovers easy. A digital photo of your client is fed to the computer, then graphic programs can show the client with different hair styles, make-up, clothing, and jewelry. It's amazing. Search the Internet for more information.

Photography service

What will I be doing?

There are more than 20,000 full-time commercial photography services in the United States. If you enjoy taking and/or developing pictures, this is an excellent home business that can offer income and satisfaction.

What do commercial photographers do? They produce and sell photographs. Some photographers specialize in portraits, cars, pets, festivals, or special events such as weddings or Bar Mitzvahs. Other photographers look for unique subjects that are artistic or humorous.

What will I need to start?

You must have the proper equipment as well as experience with cameras and photography. That's obvious. But you don't have to be an expert photographer to sell what you shoot. Many photographers go for quantity and select the best. If you shoot enough film, something's bound to come out well—as long as the lens cap is removed!

You'll need photo equipment, but professional photographers say that the most important tools they have are not the camera but lenses and lighting. Quality lenses and good lighting can make even a mediocre camera turn out quality photos.

Who will my customers be?

If you take photos of beautiful scenery, magazine or calendar publishers may be your customers. If you photograph weddings, the wedding couple or their parents will be your customers. If you photograph products, the owner or manufacturer will buy your photos.

Depending on your specialty—portraits, product, events—your potential customers can encompass a very broad range.

How much should I charge?

Commercial photographers typically have an hourly rate of $35 to $75, but price by the event or the value of the item photographed. You'll get more for photographing new or classic cars than you will for photos of traffic. Wedding and portrait photographers, for example, design a package that includes commonly requested shots at a package price. It may include staging, makeup, lighting, photography, proofs, and printing. The photographer may also offer additional shots at a set price. This makes buying easier for the customer and assures profits for the photographer.

How much will I make?

How much time you spend marketing your photography service depends on what you're selling and to whom. Plan on spending 20 to 30 percent of your time marketing your services to others.

Depending on the value of the equipment you need, plan on spending 25 to 50 percent of every dollar on overhead expenses. Simple photography using professional film-processing services requires lower overhead than buying expensive equipment and your own darkroom.

How can I get started?

The best way to get started in this business is by winning awards as an amateur photographer. Enter any legitimate contests you can, including showing your photographs at county fair judgings. Next, produce a flyer that tells others about your services and maybe even your pricing for standard packages. Finally, talk with the editor of local newspapers to promote your new business. A story on a unique aspect of your photography will greatly help you in promoting your credentials and your business.

The SIC code for commercial photography services is 7335-01.

How can I use computers to increase profits?

Photography has gone digital. Why? Because digital photographs can easily be manipulated with digital computers. "Red eye" can be fixed. Lighting can be enhanced. Skin can be improved. If you're considering photography as a home-based business, start learning about digital photography and about computer programs used to enhance digital graphics. It's the future of photography.

Public relations agency

What will I be doing?

If you love to promote people, products and events, if you are creative and friendly, this can be an excellent home business opportunity for you. A public relations agency helps clients promote themselves, their businesses, or their interests through the media and other resources. You may specialize in consulting with political candidates, special-interest groups, a new manufacturing plant, a forgotten shopping mall, or a golf tournament—all in the same week. Your work will include writing and mailing press releases, planning promotional events, contacting newspapers, radio and TV stations, appearing as a spokesperson for companies, and attending meetings with clients.

What will I need to start?

The business of promotions is mostly a craft, though there is some creativity to it. As a craft, it is learnable. You should have some experience in public relations and promotions before you consider this home business. But even if you don't, or you don't have enough, you can learn the craft as you plan your new business. In fact, you can be your first customer.

You'll need an office in your home where you can conduct business. Most PR agencies don't require a fancy office for clients. If you must meet a client in person, meet at their office or at a quiet restaurant to conduct business. Most of your contacts will be by telephone, fax, and mail. So you'll need to equip your office accordingly. You'll most likely need a computer and printer—a PR professional sends out a lot of correspondence!

Who will my customers be?

Most of your clients will be businesses, associations, or individuals. The majority will be businesses. For them you will write press releases, help journalists research stories about your client (favorable ones, of course), and develop campaigns that accent the positive traits of your client.

How much should I charge?

Public relations agencies earn good money. The typical rate is $40 to $125 an hour—the range is attributed to the variations in skill and reputation. Most public relations work is priced by the job and calculated by estimating the hours required. For example, a campaign promoting a local festival may require 60 hours of work.

At $40 an hour, the price quoted will be $2,400 plus travel and expenses. Billing is done by the month or with a portion paid at the beginning of the project and the balance in installments.

How much will I make?

A public relations agency earns a high rate but usually can't get it for more than 60 to 70 percent of available time. The rest of the time you will be promoting and administering your own business. Overhead expenses for a home-based PR agency are 20 to 40 percent of income. Your net income can range from $36,000 to $56,000 a year, once you're established.

How can I get started?

Running a PR agency is a pressure-cooker job with lots of stress, depending on your clients. Some clients are easy to work with while others can make you earn every dollar twice. And, for every easy client, there are dozens of difficult media people you must work with. If this sounds like fun, start developing your knowledge, experience, resources, contacts, and potential clients right now.

How? Be your own first client. Develop a plan for publicizing your new business and credentials to the right market. Come up with the perfect agency name and structure, get your telephone and business cards, and start making contacts. If you don't have a lot of experience in the field, volunteer to do publicity for your favorite charity, a local candidate, or a friend's business in return for references.

Contact the Public Relations Society of America (212-995-2230). The SIC code for public relations services is 8743-00.

How can I use computers to increase profits?

You can use computers to promote your business as well as your clients. The Internet opens a whole new world of prospects and contacts for publicity. For example, if you write publicity for businesses, there are many online news wires (such as *www.businesswire.com*) that distribute your releases to publications worldwide. There are even electronic clipping services (such as *www.burrelles.com*) that report back what publications picked up your release.

Real estate appraiser

What will I be doing?

Real estate appraisers check local real estate records, inspect and measure property, and calculate value based on local and industry guidelines. There are more than 30,000 real estate appraisers in the United States and many of them operate from home. A real estate appraiser gets paid for defining the value of specific real estate and may specialize in commercial real estate, residential homes, farms and acreage, or industrial property.

What will I need to start?

Surprisingly, most states don't require a real estate appraiser to be licensed as are real estate sales brokers. However, the industry still relies on professionals who have developed credentials through training and experience. Without facts and credentials, an estimate is just a guess.

So, to be a successful real estate appraiser, you'll need training and experience. Some appraisers were formerly real estate brokers or agents while others came from the mortgage side of the business. A few come from unrelated backgrounds and take college courses in real estate appraisal and marketing.

There are handbooks and computer CD-ROMs that can help you analyze market value of property. Some guides are national while others are regional or local. Your community college, local mortgage lenders, real estate board, or professional bookstores can help you find the resources you'll need.

Who will my customers be?

Potential customers for your real estate appraisal service are property sellers, buyers, agents, lenders, insurers, and others who need to know the value of a property. The actual value depends on the customer. A seller or buyer wants to know the market value while a mortgage banker wants the lending value, a more conservative figure.

Based on your background and training, you may decide to specialize in one or more types of customers or properties. Or you may find there are already too many appraisers in one area—so you focus on another where competition is less and opportunities are greater. Once you've selected your prospective customers, you can more easily find a way of telling them about your services—through advertising, telephone calls, association membership, and referrals.

How much should I charge?

A real estate appraiser typically uses a rate of $40 to $80 an hour to calculate the pricing of his or her services. In most cases, though, the price is actually quoted by the estimated time it will take to do the job. For example, a lender's appraisal that usually takes you two and a half hours at $50 an hour can be priced at $125. It may take slightly more or less time, but that's the average that you use for pricing.

How much will I make?

Once established, your appraisal service should be able to bill for 70 to 80 percent of your time, or 28 to 32 hours of a 40-hour work week. Overhead expenses for a home-based appraisal service are 15 to 35 percent of sales. So a one-person appraisal service can bring the owner a net income of $35,000 to $60,000 a year or more.

How can I get started?

You'll need credentials to compete with other appraisers. Your licensing requirements will depend on the state in which you'll be doing business. Read the ads for appraisers in your local telephone book and real estate section of area newspapers. You'll find out what associations they belong to, how much experience they have and how they attract prospective customers. You'll need a telephone with an answering service and a beeper. Or you can use a mobile phone to take your calls wherever you are.

Contact The Appraisal Institute (312-335-4100) and the National Association of Real Estate Appraisers (602-948-8000) for more information.

The SIC code for real estate appraisers is 6531-16.

How can I use computers to increase profits?

Today's real estate appraiser doesn't use a notebook. Instead, it's a notebook computer. Portable computers can not only make recording property information easier, but they can also access databases (CD or online) of public records, appraisal tables, and other resources. When done, the appraiser can print the report on the spot—or e-mail it back to the lender.

Resume writer

What will I be doing?

As a resume writer you will interview clients and write resumes and other employment documents for presentation to potential employers. You must develop or have skills in interviewing people as well as writing in commonly accepted resume styles and formats. You can work regular business hours, evenings and weekends, or on-call, depending on your commitments and preferences.

There are about 7,500 full-time resume services in the United States, with many operating from home (as I have).

What will I need to start?

You can start a resume service with a telephone, an answering machine, a computer, basic office supplies, and a small advertisement in one or more local newspapers. You should also have reference books that include sample resumes for use as guides and for clients to select from. Quality papers and other supplies are available from local or mail-order stationery suppliers.

Who will my customers be?

Your customers can include anyone who is looking for a job! Clients for your resume service are those needing help analyzing and communicating their marketable skills to employers. Because job seekers usually read the classified ads, advertising in area newspapers can draw many potential clients. Some resume writers interview clients over the telephone and mail completed resumes. Others interview face-to-face.

How much should I charge?

Resume writers typically offer standardized resume packages at set prices. The prices are based on stationery and printing costs plus an hourly rate. Hourly rates for resume writers range from $30 to $50. Depending on your skill and the complexity of the resume, it can take from one hour to several hours to prepare a resume. You can enhance your income by offering additional products or services. Some services mail resumes for their clients. Others also sell booklets on job-getting skills.

How much will I make?

A resume writer keeps about 50 to 60 percent of gross income as salary. A resume service operating 40 hours a week at an hourly rate of $35, and spending 25 percent of that time promoting the business, can earn about $1,000 a week. Net income will be $35,000 to $50,000 a year—at a fun job.

How can I get started?

Contact the Professional Association of Resume Writers (3637 Fourth St. N., St. Petersburg, FL 33704; 800-822-7279) for membership information. PARW offers a certification program, marketing aids, and a national convention.

Read *The Upstart Guide to Owning and Managing a Resume Service* by Dan Ramsey available from *www.MulliganPress.com*.

Find and hire resume writers to prepare a resume for you. Analyze how you can improve on what they do as you start your own full-time home-based resume service.

The SIC code for resume-writing services is 7338-03.

How can I use computers to increase profits?

I wish I had a computer when I operated a resume service in the early 1980s! Forms were completed by hand, the resume typewritten, and any last-minute changes meant retyping the resume. Today, computer templates streamline the process and make changes easy. In addition, computers make accessing career information online a snap. And Web pages can be used to market your services to a wider audience.

Secretarial/word-processing service

What will I be doing?

There are nearly 10,000 full-time professional secretarial services in the United States, with about half of them also offering computerized word-processing services.

What does a secretarial service do? It performs professional office services (typing, data entry, dictation, filing) for clients. In a typical day, the service may mail out 500 brochures, transcribe an accountant's dictation into letters, and pick up a client's mail at the post office.

What will I need to start?

This business sells your secretarial skills to people who need them. So your secretarial skills must be advanced and efficient. Your service may specialize in one or two skills such as typing or dictation. If so, develop your skills and experience, earning certification if you can. You want your customers to have a reason to select your services over those of another.

You'll be on top of your competition if you keep up with the latest technology in computers and accompanying software. The more you know about various software programs, for example, the more clients you can take on. Other equipment that will give your service the edge includes fax machines and modems, which allow for the electronic transfer of files and mail. One successful secretarial service is operated from home by a woman who produces and delivers documents electronically after her children are off to school. With her computer and online services, she can offer one day service while working her own hours.

Who will my customers be?

Most of your customers will be other businesses. They may be professional offices that have an overload of work or you may provide services that the employed staff cannot. Once you've decided what kind of services you will offer, finding customers will be easier. If you specialize in medical transcription, contact medical offices in your area. If your specialty is legal dictation, try law offices. If you are adept at typing college papers, advertise where college students will learn about your services.

How much should I charge?

The hourly rate for secretarial and word-processing services ranges from $25 to $45. Depending on the services you offer and the type of client you serve, you may offer all services on a per-hour price. Other secretarial services price by the word, the page, the job, or other component. A few are priced on retainer, furnishing a specific number of hours each week or month to clients under contract.

How much will I make?

Your established secretarial business will be able to bill at least 75 percent of your time to clients. The rest will be devoted to marketing and finding new customers. During the first few months, your service will require up to half of your time for marketing.

Overhead expenses for a secretarial and/or word-processing service depend on many factors including what equipment you need to do your job. The typical range is 20 to 40 percent for overhead expenses including taxes. That means you can probably keep 60 to 80 cents of every dollar you bring in. An efficient secretarial service can offer the owner a net income of $35,000 to $50,000 a year or more.

How can I get started?

First, identify your potential customers and learn what secretarial services they need. Second, develop a flyer that describes your services and their benefits and that invites the prospect's call for a free consultation or pricing. If your services are standard, include your prices for these services. Finally, get the word out. Let others know what you do and how you can help them. Ask friends, relatives, former employers, and businesspeople you know for referrals.

The SIC code for secretarial services is 7338-05 and for word-processing services the SIC code is 7338-02.

How can I use computers to increase profits?

Today's secretarial service cannot survive without a computer—or two. Documents come in and go out as electronic files. Editing and revision are performed on the computer. The majority of secretarial services use the most popular word processing program today, Microsoft Word. However, many have other programs as well for clients who prefer them. Some secretarial services have expanded to do simple desktop publishing of brochures, fliers, and other sales collateral.

Shopper publisher

What will I be doing?

The "shopper" is an advertising publication that has been around for nearly 50 years but had its heyday between 1965 and 1975. This publication sprang up around the country, challenging newspapers for advertisers. It did so by offering free circulation and low-cost ads. In fact, the classified ad rate was often 5 cents a word, hence the name "nickel ads."

Inflation has increased ad rates to 10 to 25 cents a word, but the concept is still profitable: low-cost, high-circulation advertising. If you have experience selling or producing print advertisements, developing a shopper for your town or region may be a lucrative home-based business for you. Once you publish the shopper, you will have to see to its distribution, either by mail or by displaying it at local stores so customers can help themselves to it.

What will I need to start?

To attract readers, most newspapers limit advertising to less than 50 percent of the available space. Shoppers don't use the same limit. In fact, many shoppers are 100 percent advertising. Others use a feature story on the front page to draw readers to the advertising-filled pages.

The greatest skill you'll need to publish a shopper is salesmanship. You will make most of your money from the commercial display ads in the publication. Small classified ads bring income, but the expense of gathering and billing for them eats up most of the profit. Learn to sell display ads and your shopper has a greater chance of success.

You will also need a computer and some desktop publishing programs for the design and layout of the ads. If your budget is small, consider starting as many of the early shoppers did: simply cut ads from newspapers and sell placement in your shopper to the advertisers. The layout work is done for you. The classified ads can be produced with a typewriter with carbon ribbon.

You'll also need a printer. Smaller shoppers can be produced on a photocopy machine or quick-print press. Larger shoppers are published on newsprint by a Web press (sometimes by the competing newspaper!).

Who will my customers be?

Customers for your shopper advertising will be small businesses and individuals wanting to sell or buy products and services. Most frequent advertisers are used-car dealers, second-hand stores, and small discount stores.

You can get classified ads by calling up those who advertise in the local newspaper's classified section and telling them your circulation and ad rates.

How much should I charge?

Advertising is sold by the column inch. A shopper may have four to six columns of classified ads on a page. A column inch is one column wide and one inch high. A page with five columns of 15 inches has 75 column-inches per page. If your customer's ad is two columns wide by 5 inches high or 10 column-inches, and your rate is $4 a column-inch, the ad will cost $40.

You can calculate your column-inch rate by figuring costs, but you will also need to compare it with the rate the newspaper and other shoppers in the area charge the same advertisers.

How much will I make?

Your printing bill will take one-third to one-half of your income. A home-based shopper publisher will typically have a net income of 30 to 50 percent of gross income. So to earn a net income of $30,000 a year you'll need a gross income from advertising of $60,000 to $90,000 a year.

How can I get started?

First, study your potential competition. Pick up local newspapers, shoppers, and any other publications that carry local advertisements. Study the publications and ads carefully. Contact the publications to find out what advertising rates are. Calculate income for an issue.

Second, talk with potential advertisers to find out whether they would support another publication. Are they willing to sign a contract in exchange for a discount? If so, you may find the cash you need to start.

The SIC code for shopper publications is 2741-09.

How can I use computers to increase profits?

Shoppers are popular because they save readers money. That means the publisher must also save money to make money. Computer publishing programs have streamlined publishing, making it easier for one person to take the ad, enter it into the computer, publish it, bill it, and collect money using a single program.

Transcription service

What will I be doing?

If you take dictation, type like the wind, and know technical terms, you can offer a transcription service from your home. A transcription service translates spoken words into written words for medical, legal, editorial, and other employers. Some transcription service go a step further, summarizing transcripts for easier reading.

What will I need to start?

A transcription service today requires a computer with a word processor. It also requires transcription equipment, such as a Dictaphone. Some prefer small cassettes. In any case, you'll need equipment to listen and transcribe.

You will also need to know the "language" of your client. Medical and legal terms are like a foreign language to those unfamiliar with them. You must know these words and how to spell them if you will be transcribing them. Fortunately, there are books and even computer software programs that will help. There are also courses you can take to help learn these terms.

Who will my customers be?

Your customers will be doctors, lawyers, editors, and other professionals who prefer to dictate than write their words. Most do it for efficiency or convenience. You may transcribe an attorney's recorded notes into a contract or a to-do list. You may transcribe a doctor's recorded comments into a medical record. Or you may transcribe an interview between a writer and a famous celebrity for an upcoming book.

How much should I charge?

Transcription services establish a rate of $25 to $60 an hour, but price by the line, page, or document. The price may be $1 a page or $30 for a client report. To price by units, select the typical unit for your field, estimate the average time to transcribe and process, then price it accordingly.

How much will I make?

Your established transcription service will probably require less than 20 percent of your time for marketing. Until then, you may spend as much as half of your time selling your service to others.

Overhead expenses depend on the equipment you need and your travel time, if any, between jobs. If all dictation is delivered to you, your overhead will be lower than if you have to travel to your client's location. Expect overhead expenses ranging from 20 to 40 percent. So net income for a full-time transcription service can range from $25,000 to $50,000 a year or more.

How can I get started?

First, build your skills. You will be paid for efficiency and accuracy. If you work slowly or make mistakes, you will lose business. Make sure you have the needed skills before you start your transcription service.

Second, contact potential customers, interviewing them about their transcription needs. What services would they like that they're not getting now?

Third, define and promote your business. Focus on a specific type of transcription and customer, then go after them.

The SIC code for transcription services is 7389-17.

How can I use computers to increase profits?

Transcribers have come to rely on computers to simplify their process. They not only use word processing programs to enter information, they also use professional dictionaries (legal, medical, business) to verify spelling accuracy. Then they use computers to publish transcripts in a variety of forms. Finally, computers track projects, manage customers, and promote their business.

Translation service

What will I be doing?

Are you fluent in a language other than English? Can you translate or interpret for others? If so, you may be able to offer a profitable translation service from your home.

A translation service interprets documents and conversations between users of two or more languages. Such a service may also translate correspondence, newspapers, magazines, and other materials.

What will I need to start?

Most translation services specialize in two or more languages such as English and French. Some services specialize in a group of related languages such as Asian.

So you must have proficiency in at least two languages. You may prefer to translate written or spoken words. A literary translator can usually work at home in his or her spare time while a vocal translator may be required to be on-call for conference telephone calls or even travel.

You will probably need some tools and equipment to help you, such as language dictionaries and tapes, and current books in the second language to keep you informed about changes in the language and new terms that have entered it.

Who will my customers be?

Your customers will be international companies, individuals, students, and publishers. For example, an international manufacturer may want you to translate product literature into the language of a new market. Or a buyer may be visiting from a foreign country and require vocal translation services while meeting with the manufacturer. Individuals may need letters from relatives in the "old country" translated. Foreign students studying in a nearby college may need help with English. Publishers may have a book for translation into English before publication.

In most cases, letting others know of your skills and experience with foreign languages will draw business to you. However, you will need to make the effort to inform others through business cards, fliers, and telephone calls.

How much should I charge?

A translation service sets a rate of $30 to $75 an hour depending on proficiency, type of translation, and whether travel is required. A translator of books at home will typically earn less than a vocal translator who must travel to customer sites. The travel time won't be paid at the full rate, but the translator should be compensated for the extra efforts of travel.

Translation services price by the hour, the page, the class, the publication's length, or other factors, but you'll need to calculate your prices based on your hourly rates, regardless of how you quote prices to your clients.

How much will I make?

Your experienced translation service will bill 80 to 90 percent of your time with the rest spent on marketing and administration. To get your business off the ground, you may need to spend as much as half your time promoting your business and even doing volunteer translation to develop credentials and references.

Overhead expenses for translation services include a telephone, office supplies, and reference materials. Expect overhead costs of 10 to 30 percent for a home-based translation service. A successful translation service in a metropolitan area can earn $35,000 to $60,000 a year or more for the owner, depending on local need, competition, and qualifications.

How can I get started?

First, you must be proficient at your translation language. If possible, write a book or get some certification in that language to use as a recommendation. Second, make sure you are proficient in your *own* language! To translate well you must know two languages well. Also, let others know about your skills and service. Depending on the language and type of translation you prefer, contact businesses, importers, exporters, students, publishers, and others who must cross the language barrier.

Yes, even translation services have a SIC code: 7389-20.

How can I use computers to increase profits?

Can computers be used in the translation process? Yes! In fact, there are many translation programs that do the "shovel work." That is, the programs read the data file and make a first attempt at translating the document. Then the professional edits it to catch things that the software could not.

Video-production service

What will I be doing?

The more than 16,000 video-production businesses in the United States offer a wide variety of services. They video weddings, Little League games, children's birthday parties, bowling tournaments, grand openings, and other special events. Some produce local commercials. Others transfer 8mm film and photos to video for customers. A few produce instructional tapes or documentaries for sale to television or directly to consumers. Most have fun at what they do.

What will I need to start?

There's more to producing a video than pushing the button on the side of the camera. Lots more. Producing quality video images that can be sold to others requires a knowledge of cameras, subjects, lighting, and production techniques. It also requires video equipment for taping, editing, mixing, dubbing, and copying tapes.

Who will my customers be?

Most video services offer a variety of services to individuals, companies and associations. Others focus on one type of service or customer, especially in areas crowded with video-production services. A successful video service in the Northwest specializes in video taping antique and classic car shows, auctions, and other events for clubs and car owners. Another service in California videos school events such as sports games and graduations.

How much should I charge?

Because video equipment is expensive, most video-production services need a lot of money to start. However, a few start with rented or borrowed equipment. Because of the costs, a video-production service will set prices based on a studio rate of $50 to $150 an hour.

Pricing is set by the estimated time it will take to video the event and edit it in the studio. For example, video taping a high school graduation that requires two hours of taping, an hour of setup and takedown, two hours of editing, and another three hours to make 20 copies—a total of 8 hours at $60 an hour—will charge $24 a copy plus the cost of the tape. If the event is done on speculation, not knowing how many tapes will be sold, the videos will be priced by the minimum number of tapes you estimate will sell.

How much will I make?

Expenses for a video-production business can eat up 40 to 50 percent of gross income. A business that sells $100,000 in services can offer the owner an annual income of $40,000 to $50,000 before taxes. Most video services take a year or more to build to this level. Once established, an aggressive service can increase gross income by 25 to 50 percent a year or more. If overhead expenses are managed well and competition is aggressively faced, the owner can expect a very profitable business.

How can I get started?

Learn your business! It takes more than a camera to make a profitable video service. Study the market and your potential competitors for ways you can do the job more efficiently and profitably. Look for groups unserved by video services in your area. For example, consider specializing in video taping Bar Mitzvahs or outdoor weddings or college wrestling tournaments or whatever has many customers and few competitors.

Read the video trade magazines available at larger photo shops for opportunities, ideas, and the latest equipment. Start setting up a studio and office in your home, depending on what type of video production you will do. Develop your video-production service as a spare time venture until it is profitable, then consider going full-time. Have fun at what you do!

The SIC code for video-production services is 7812-11.

How can I use computers to increase profits?

Like other forms of photography, video is now digital. Not only is digital video photography clearer than analog, it is also easier to edit. Images can be enhanced, digital effects can be applied, titling is easier, and distribution becomes easier. There's a price: digital video equipment is more expensive. But the quality and the flexibility can help you increase your profits.

Wholesaler

What will I be doing?

You don't have to have a huge warehouse and sales staff to be a wholesaler. All you really need are product sources and retailers. Wholesalers are necessary because most manufacturers make zillions of one product and don't want to mess with selling four of them to a mom-and-pop store. If you can buy a couple hundred for resale, you could be a wholesaler.

Wholesaler of what? That depends. If you have knowledge or contacts within a specific industry, you can wholesale products from that industry to retailers. For example, you can wholesale specialized auto parts or pita bread or natural herbs in bulk. Stay away from more common products handled by large wholesalers.

What will I need to start?

First, you need a product to wholesale and a retail group to sell to. If you have both, great! But most small wholesalers have more knowledge of either one or the other. They may have experience working for retailers and know their needs. Or they may have an understanding of one or more manufacturers or product lines and want to wholesale them to retailers.

You may also need some storage space, but it doesn't have to be in your home. You can rent a portion or entire warehouse. Or you can specialize in selling products that are shipped directly from the manufacturer to the retailer—but be careful as one or the other might decide to work directly and cut you out of the picture.

Who will my customers be?

Your customers will be retail businesses who need smaller quantities of one or more product than the manufacturer wants to mess with. Which retailers depend on what you're wholesaling. You may be a floral wholesaler buying flowers in quantity from large growers and selling them to retailers. Or your customers may be specialty grocery stores that want products they can't get from their primary wholesaler, such as imported curry, canned snails, or real sourdough yeast.

How much should I charge?

Wholesalers are paid by commission on the value of the products sold. It's typically a percent of the retail price such as 5 to 15 percent. A case of spices that the importer prices at $40 may sell at $45 to $60 to a specialty store that marks it up to $100 or more. You don't make as much money per-case as the retailer does, but you make it up in volume selling to many stores.

How much will I make?

Overhead expenses for your wholesale operation can range from 10 to 35 percent of income depending on whether you have to warehouse your products. A wholesaler's net income, once established, can be $25,000 to $80,000 or more, with most one-person, home-based operations on the lower end of the scale for the first few years.

How can I get started?

Look around for a specialty item or line that isn't being offered efficiently or widely in your area. It may involve a specialized food or product. If you were raised or spent time in a foreign country, consider what products you know about that may do well here in a specific market. You may find both a resource and a market for authentic Korean kimchee or fresh Mexican tamale husks. Consider visiting specialty retailers in your area, asking the owner or manager what products they would like to buy wholesale that they're not getting now. With enough potential, you could be their new wholesaler.

The SIC code for general wholesalers is 5199-77. However, wholesalers of specific products have other SIC codes.

How can I use computers to increase profits?

Wholesaling is an information game. The more you know about your products, your suppliers, your buyers, and the marketplace, the more you will profit. That's where the computer shines: gathering and tracking information. Most successful wholesalers have Web sites for selling their products. Others rely heavily on electronic mail or e-mail. If you haven't done so already, start taking classes and reading books on how to conduct business—wholesale and retail— on the Internet. It's called e-commerce and it's the direction that business is moving.

6 Best Service Businesses

Aerobics studio

What will I be doing?

The fitness craze continues. In fact, it is big business. If you enjoy helping people work toward fitness and weight-loss goals in a social atmosphere—while keeping fit yourself—consider managing a full-time aerobics studio in your home. That's right, in your home. You can provide the facilities for classes or coordinate the use of an outside studio from your home.

What will I need to start?

The first requirement for a full-time home-based aerobics studio is an interest in fitness and a strong desire to help others. You'll also need knowledge and skills. Start an aerobics studio after you've been a regular customer of a studio for a year or more. You'll then understand what customers expect from a studio, what is available, and how to reach new customers. You'll probably have the knowledge and skills to make your studio a success.

You'll need other resources as well, including a space to hold the class and some equipment—such as exercise mats and music equipment. Don't worry that your location may not be on a major highway. Many successful aerobics studios operate in a garage and draw people who live within jogging distance. A few manage the studio from home but hold classes in a church basement, rent a room in a commercial gymnasium, or even teach classes on-site at a local business.

Who will my customers be?

Customers for your aerobics studio include both students and instructors. You can specialize in organizing exercise classes for the elderly, rent your studio to aerobics teachers who find their own students, give lessons yourself, or all of the above.

Finding your customers will be easier once you've decided how you want to manage and run your studio. Look around to discover what customers are not being served well. Ask your friends who are into aerobics and other fitness programs. Then learn what your potential customers have in common aside from exercise. Maybe they go to a specialized health food store in your area or read a certain local publication.

How much should I charge?

The hourly rate for your studio will depend on many factors. Typical rate is $40 to $75 an hour for the studio depending on size, location, and equipment. You'll get the higher rate if you take on some of the marketing yourself and set up your own classes. The lower rate will be for teachers who sign a contract with you for a specific amount of time.

How much will I make?

The costs of operating an aerobics studio are minimal, especially if it is located in your home. You will have costs of furnishings, extra electricity for lighting, some added insurance costs, advertising costs, and a few other expenses. Of course, expenses will be higher if you rent a building somewhere else.

Once established, only 10 to 20 percent of your time will be needed for management and marketing. Within a year you should be able to keep your studio booked up months in advance with little effort. Your overhead costs will be 20 to 40 percent of income depending on expenses. So a studio that is booked 30 hours a week at $50 an hour with 30 percent overhead costs will net you $1,050 a week.

How can I get started?

To start a successful aerobics studio you must first know who your best customers will be. Maybe they are your friends and acquaintances. Maybe they are members of a fitness teachers' group. Talk with them. Learn what they want in a studio that they aren't getting now. Then decide whether your home or apartment is the best location for the classes or whether you should rent a building. If so, find out where. Begin looking for an opportunity today and within a few weeks you may be able to help others stay fit in your aerobics studio.

How can I use computers to increase profits?

Aerobic studios use computers to track enrollment, schedule classes, bill customers, produce newsletters and class fliers, and for time management. A package such as Microsoft Office can do many of these chores. So can the less expensive Microsoft Works or other packages. Or you may find individual programs that better fit your needs. Trade publications for aerobic services will include ads for useful software.

Bed-and-breakfast operator

What will I be doing?

Bed-and-breakfast (B&B) establishments continue to be a popular home business. Unfortunately, not all such establishments are profitable.

A bed-and-breakfast inn is in the business of serving others. B&Bs offer private room rentals catering to overnight and longer stays, especially weekend travelers. Most serve some food to guests. Typically, B&B operators are owners of a large house, often one that embodies a sense of history in some way, whether it's in the actually history of the home, in architectural style, or in the surrounding attractions. The home must have separate rooms or apartments that can be rented out to guests who typically stay a few nights or for a vacation. Running a B&B requires a lot of work—from housekeeping, preparing and serving breakfast, to answering questions about local sites and attractions.

What will I need to start?

The key to a successful bed-and-breakfast inn is not necessarily the house itself, but the location. Popular B&Bs are usually located in resort or destination areas, or historic districts in a major city. A classic B&B in an industrial town may be unprofitable, while a simple unit in a popular resort may be booked up into the next century.

Besides location, B&B guests seek ambiance and charm. Whether it's a Victorian dollhouse, an elegant English manor, or a rustic mountain retreat, your customers demand more comfort and character than they would find at the nearby budget motel. Your rates will be set accordingly.

In addition, you will need some experience or knowledge of the hospitality industry. Your guests may sleep in each morning, but you won't be able to. Be prepared for lots of cleaning and cooking— remember the "breakfast" part of bed-and-breakfast! Depending on what type of B&B you establish, you may offer simple pastries purchased locally or prepare a full country breakfast from scratch.

Who will my customers be?

Most people who stay at a bed-and-breakfast inn are destination travelers. They have come to your town for recreation and relaxation. They don't want a traditional motel. They would prefer staying with a local family or couple. That's you.

How can you find customers? Be one. If you now live in a big city, visit B&B's in the historic neighborhoods or look at the resorts in your area. If you live in a resort, consider the cities that it serves. Find resort guides and other publications on the area that advertise B&Bs. Study them. Visit them. Find out what's successful, then do it.

How much should I charge?

Rates for B&Bs vary widely from less than $100 to $300 a night and more. Much depends on where your B&B is, what area motels are getting, and what additional ambiance and services you provide. Many B&Bs start with a rate that is double the typical local motel rate. Of course, your rate will vary depending upon the high and low travel season in your area.

How much will I make?

A small B&B can earn the owners a profit (including salary) of $40,000 to $100,000 a year for full-time efforts. You can hire help or, as many B&B managers do, hire your family. You will also profit from a zero-commute time.

Living where you work can also be a liability, keeping you from getting out and enjoying your resort town and area attractions. Some B&B operators trade time with those who own units in other resorts. Kind of a busman's holiday.

How can I get started?

The "perfect" home business requires a large investment in a house, so you will need lots of money and/or credit to start a successful B&B. Sometimes you can buy or even lease a unit from someone who is tired of the business. In any case, get experience in the hospitality field, especially with B&Bs if you can.

In addition, consider joining trade associations where you can learn from the successes and mistakes of others. Three worth considering are: American Bed-and-Breakfast Association (800-769-2468); Professional Association of Innkeepers International (805-569-1853); and National Bed-and-Breakfast Association (203-847-6196).

The SIC code for bed-and-breakfast inns is 7011-07.

How can I use computers to increase profits?

Bed-and-breakfast businesses are based on service. Computers and software can enhance service by keeping track of reservations. They are also useful for managing the checkbook for income and expenses. In addition, desktop publishing programs can help you produce great looking brochures, breakfast menus, place cards, business cards, and many other promotional materials.

Caregiver

What will I be doing?

Health is one of the most important aspects of life. Most people would trade wealth for health. You can be an important part of this industry while working as a caregiver.

A caregiver provides healthcare services most often in the home of the client. Care may involve simply making sure the patient's basic needs are met.

What will I need to start?

To start your caregiver business you'll first need a strong desire to serve others. Without it, some of the chores are more difficult. You will also need a basic understanding of the patient's health problems and how to assist. A degree, certification, or advanced courses in nursing will help you. Without a background or certification in medical services or nursing, your opportunities and potential income will be more limited. You will only be able to provide the basic services of dressing, bathing, etc.

Typically, special equipment and medications will be provided by others. They may also provide a bed and clothing. What you need to start depends somewhat on the type of care you will provide, whether full- or part-time, whether in your home or that of your patient and other factors.

Who will my customers be?

Who hires independent caregivers? Insurance companies, hospitals, nursing homes, care management services, and individuals. Your ultimate customer will be the patient.

To find customers, let government and private health care organizations in your area know that you are offering in-home care and advertise your services in local newspapers.

How much should I charge?

A caregiver who is simply offering companion services without medical assistance will charge less for lower skill requirements. In this case, the caregiver may charge $12 to $18 a day, less if there are more than three clients being cared for at any one time. Typically, what you get for health care services will depend on what others are paying. That is, a hospital or insurance company may offer $70 a day per patient for in-home health care. Or a care management service may pay $85 a week for a specific number of visits. Billing will be by the week or month.

How much will I make?

The income you make as a caregiver is small, but you can have more than one patient at a time. Your income as a caregiver depends on your number and type of clients, their specific needs, how much actual time your business requires, your abilities and skills, and what the local market will pay. Income can range from $15,000 to $45,000 or more a year.

How can I get started?

First, check with government health services in your area to learn the requirements for operating a home care business. Some states have stricter laws than others. You may be required to have your home certified. You may also need to take some classes.

Call Mentor Clinical Care (800-388-5150).

How can I use computers to increase profits?

Caregivers who use their home for helping clients have many opportunities for writing off legitimate expenses to reduce their tax obligation. It starts with good recordkeeping. QuickBooks, for example, can be set up to track income from the state and clients, track client-specific expenses, and prorate general expenses to your clients based on days each month they live in your home.

Cart/kiosk sales

What will I be doing?

Cart peddlers have sold their wares from movable carts for hundreds of years. They have sold food, novelties, flowers, and other impulse products out of carts that can be moved from site to site or stationary booths or kiosks. While in the past being a cart peddler involved pushing a heavy load of merchandise through the streets in sun, snow, or rain, you can enjoy the benefits of this occupation without suffering the weather. Most cart or kiosk stations are found in climate-controlled indoor malls or other public places.

What will I need to start?

Location is an important part of starting a cart/kiosk business. A poor location will bring few customers and little sales. Fortunately, it's easier to move a kiosk or cart to a new location than to move a retail store or restaurant. But you can't just set up your cart anywhere you want. You will probably need a city or county permit as well as permission from the owners of the property where you place your mini-business. Depending on what and how you sell, you may also need lighting, signage, a cash register, inventory and, of course, a cart or kiosk, which you can either purchase or rent.

Who will my customers be?

Your customers will be those who want to buy specific products or services at a location convenient to them. One successful cart operator sold hot dogs and sausages from a steam cart that he kept in the corner of a warehouse. Just before lunch, he would roll it to his regular location, start it up and begin serving. Customers came to him.

Your cart or kiosk must be located where your customers are most likely to be, such as on a busy city street or in a shopping mall. You can operate your business full- or part-time, year-round or seasonally. By watching when and where you make sales, you can determine the best location and times for your business.

How much should I charge?

You will be charging by the product or service you sell, but should calculate your time at $20 to $40 an hour depending on the cost of your equipment and its operation. Many cart and kiosk operators use a simple multiplier to mark up products to their retail price. Food carts usually mark prices up 300 to 400 percent of wholesale. For example, a hot dog, bun, and condiments cost 50 cents in materials and sell for $1.50 to $2 as a finished product. Products sold from a cart or kiosk are typically marked up 200 to 300 percent from wholesale. A $4 wholesale necklace is sold at $8 to $12—or $7.99 to $11.99. The markup is less because no preparation is required.

How much will I make?

How much you make with your cart or kiosk depends on many factors, the greatest of which is the location. If you get to keep 50 cents of every dollar you take in (after all expenses), a cart that sells an average of $100 an hour (a hot dog a minute!) will give you $50 for the hour. A kiosk with an average income of $35 an hour over the day will give you $17.50 an hour.

Some carts and kiosks pay a percentage of rent to the owner of their location. The typical rate is 10 to 20 percent. A jewelry cart that sells $600 in merchandise a day will be paying $60 to $120 for the day's rent.

How can I get started?

To start your cart or kiosk business, first do some market research. Look around your community for successful cart operators and study them. A few hours or days of study will help you estimate their income, expenses, and profits. Buy something from them to learn more. Pick a slow time and they may talk with you about their business.

Next, pick a product. It must be something that will sell well, but isn't already oversold at your location. Finally, find the best location. Add a cart or kiosk, some products or services and have fun.

Contact Westrock Vending Vehicles (516-666-5252) and the Great Gazebo (517-332-6126) for more information.

How can I use computers to increase profits?

Most kiosk sales units offer instant credit card approval for purchases. To do so, many use a computer and software for entering and approving the sale. A telephone line to the kiosk is also needed for instant approval. Order-entry software can help schedule clerks, determine which days and hours are the most profitable, help with product inventory, and many other tasks. Of course, hot dog stands and similar low-ticket sales are typically cash only. Even so, you must track income and expenses with a computer at home.

Catering service

What will I be doing?

Catering is a popular business with more than 46,000 catering businesses existing in the United States. What does a caterer do? He or she purchases, prepares, delivers, and serves food for special events. If you enjoy preparing food and making others happy, a catering service may be a good home-based business for you.

What will I need to start?

First, you'll need to check with local and state health departments to determine what licenses, permits, and certifications are required to operate a catering service. If you prepare your own food, your kitchen will probably need to be certified as a commercial kitchen. Some caterers work around this by renting restaurant kitchens during the mid-morning and mid-afternoon slow periods.

You'll also need utensils, delivery and service tools, as well as a source of food and supplies. If you're renting a commercial kitchen, some of these requirements will be available.

Who will my customers be?

Customers for your catering service include individuals who want to give parties, companies needing to feed employees for a sales meeting or picnic, as well as groups and associations for meetings or seminars.

One successful caterer began her business as an employee of a popular restaurant. She contracted with the owners to pay them 25 percent of any catering she did if she could use the kitchen during the off-hours. Both profited from the partnership.

How much should I charge?

The hourly rate for catering services is typically $25 to $75, depending on many factors. The greater the caterer's skills and reputation, the higher the hourly rate. Pricing of catered events is typically per-person. A catered company picnic may be priced at $6 per person while an elaborate formal dinner may be priced at $45 per person. The caterer's hourly rate is added to the cost of food and preparation to establish the base price.

How much will I make?

Your catering service can be very profitable once you've learned how to operate it efficiently. Waste is the greatest enemy of profits in the food service industry. Lower the waste and you will increase profits.

One successful caterer specialized in catering weddings, planning one on each of the days of the weekend. She charged $8 per person with a 50-person minimum. After paying for food, preparation, delivery, and service, she earned about $22 an hour for her time. The 14 hours she spent on her business over each weekend netted her about $16,000 a year—after taxes! As word-of-mouth spread and her client list grew, she was able to develop her weekend catering business into a full-time venture.

How can I get started?

To be successful in the catering business, develop your food preparation and cooking skills, learn how to buy and store foods, and learn to minimize waste. I suggest you read this book: *Catering: Start and Run a Money-Making Business* by Judy Richards (TAB/McGraw-Hill), currently out of print but available from *www.MulliganPress.com*.

The SIC code for catering services is 5812-12.

How can I use computers to increase profits?

Caterers must track job income and expenses down to the olive. This requires good recordkeeping software (refer to Chapter 3). In addition, caterers need to print menus. Inexpensive (under $100) desktop publishing software can be used for this. Or most word processing programs can do a decent menu or flyer with columns.

Childcare

What will I be doing?

Children are our future. They can also be your business. As a home-based childcare provider, you will be responsible for providing care, entertainment, and meals or snacks for preschool children in your home.

There are more than 60,000 full-time childcare centers in the United States and many times more people who care for one or two children in their home or babysit at the children's home. Though the income per child is moderate, caring for more than one child at a time can help you make a good living.

What will I need to start?

To care for children you must really care *about* them. If you have experience and/or training in child development, you're off to a good start. You'll also need to have adequate space in a home that is child-friendly as well as accessible to parents who need to drop off their children. Your childcare business will also require licensing, inspection, and certification, depending on local regulations. If you prepare food and serve it to children, you may need additional licensing or certification. Of course, you'll also need toys and other items to entertain and keep children busy.

Who will my customers be?

Your customers will typically be working parents and grandparents of preschool-age children. You may also decide to offer your services to local businesses who will then offer it to their employees. To reach potential customers, let your friends and neighbors know about your new business. Contact local schools, place a small service ad in the newspaper, and publicize your business locally.

How much should I charge?

You will price your childcare services by the hour and the service provided. That is, you may charge $2 an hour for four or more hours a day, $2.50 an hour for less than four hours a day and an additional $3 for a meal. You will then add these prices up to give customers a single price, such as $105 a week for five nine-hour days including meals. Check prices of local day-care centers to determine a reasonable price for your services, and set your prices accordingly.

How much will I make?

Most of what you make with your childcare service you get to keep. Overhead expenses include toys, meals, and incidentals. The greatest expense is already paid: that of your home. In fact, you will be able to deduct the costs of the part of your home used for childcare. You will use IRS *Form 8829, Expenses for Business Use of Your Home*, which includes a special calculation for day-care facilities.

How can I get started?

Start your childcare service by learning more about local requirements. Check with state and local government offices to find out which regulate day-care centers. Next, begin planning your business, how you will operate it and how much you will charge. Finally, let others know about your new business.

Contact the National Association for Family Child Care (800-359-3817).

The SIC code for childcare services is 8351-01.

How can I use computers to increase profits?

Many home-based day-care centers take over the home. Owners live upstairs and the kids get the downstairs. And so much of what goes into the home for operation, maintenance, and repair is tax-deductible as business expenses. Again, that means good recordkeeping. The easiest way of doing so is with checking software (see Chapter 3) that categorizes and reports income and expenses. In addition, a database program can help manage scheduling and enrollment.

Collection service

What will I be doing?

Most people pay their bills on time. When they don't, a collection service may be hired. Collection services assist businesses in collecting money owed to them by their customers while encouraging a continuing relationship. This usually entails mail and telephone correspondence as your primary tools for reaching delinquent customers.

Many of the people who operate successful collection services aren't those with pristine credit. In fact, many are those who have had debt problems in the past and know how to help others get out of debt. They offer a useful service to both businesses and consumers, and get paid well for doing so.

What will I need to start?

To start your own collection service you'll first need an understanding of the credit and collection side of business. Books on the subject will help, but practical experience in either or both sides of credit will give you an edge. You'll need "thick skin," self-respect, and respect for your clients. You will also need a telephone and some office supplies.

You don't have to be a lawyer, but you will have to learn about the laws of credit and collection. There are many books and pamphlets available on what you can and cannot do as a collection service.

Who will my customers be?

Businesses with overdue accounts receivable will need you to help them collect. In most cases, the business has already tried unsuccessfully to collect on the account. By the time you get the account, there may be bad feelings on both sides or the customer may have thought the bill was canceled. Your customers will be businesses, but without their customers—those who owe money—you won't be paid.

Some collection services specialize in healthcare, child support, small business, retail credit, or other areas. If you have special knowledge or experience in one of these areas, you may be able to collect bad debts where others can't. This is a good selling point to your customers.

How much should I charge?

Most collection services don't get paid by the hour. If they did, the range would be $30 to $60, depending on the type and size of debts and the success of the collector. If you don't collect, you don't get paid.

How much should you charge for your collection services? The typical range is 25 to 50 percent of the value of the debt. A collection service that gets the debtor to pay a $1,000 medical bill will earn $250 to $500 depending on the age of the bill and the agreement with the business. Most debts are for a few hundred dollars. Some collection services don't use the telephone, but rely on legal-sounding letters in order to collect.

How much will I make?

Income from a collection service depends on your skills to find collectible debts and get them paid. So income can range from $0 to $1,000 a week. This is not a job for everyone; it requires a lot of tenacity to turn it into a profitable source of income. Within a few months you'll learn whether this is a business you will enjoy and profit from.

How can I get started?

Consider starting your business with a single business account and a specific group of debts to test your skills and interests. Then expand as you wish. If you have credit and collection experience, your learning curve will be shorter and your profits will come faster than without this valuable experience.

Most important, remember that the service you provide is valuable to both your customers and theirs.

Contact the American Collectors' Association (612-926-6547).

How can I use computers to increase profits?

Collectors can be more efficient by using computer software that tracks accounts, prints out collection letters, and manages other recordkeeping tasks. Software can also help you determine which collection methods work and which don't. In addition, computers are useful for research on the Internet.

Companion to the elderly

What will I be doing?

Everybody needs a friend. If you enjoy helping others, especially older people, you can establish a home business as a companion to elderly or disabled people. You can operate this business from
your home, visiting clients at their homes or by telephone.

What will I need to start?

Many of the elderly, particularly those who are invalid, need
someone around to talk with or to listen to them. They may need
help writing letters and paying bills or remembering to take medica-
tion. To start your business you will need patience, compassion, and
a listening ear. You will also need transportation to and from your
clients' homes, but public transportation can be used if nothing else
is available. Some experience with the elderly, such as a parent or
grandparent, or even volunteer work at a nursing or retirement home,
will provide you with greater understanding of your clients.

Who will my customers be?

Your customers will be the elderly, the children of elderly, social
services, and health organizations. Or you may be hired by a nursing home to make regular visits to individual guests.

To find customers, check the local telephone book for government social services for the elderly. A few telephone calls and a visit
will tell you much about what services are now available and how
you can fit in. You may also get referrals.

How much should I charge?

Your fees will be based on an hourly rate of $15 to $25, depending on the number of patients, location, and your unbillable time.
Most companion services work to establish clients that live close to
each other, such as in a retirement community or older neighborhood, to reduce commuting time and increase referral business. With
efficiency, a companion can spend two half-hour or four 15-minute
sessions a month with a client for less than $30 a month. For some
clients, that will be a lot of money. But if you can help them with
cleaning or paying bills, your cost will be well worth it to them.

How much will I make?

A full-time companion service can earn $200 to $500 a week working
with a number of regular clients. You won't get rich financially, but

you will be giving others a much-needed service: friendship and companionship.

How can I get started?

Gain experience by visiting or spending time with elderly and disabled friends. Visit them regularly to determine what they need, how often, and when. Once you've decided to start the business, ask for referrals.

How can I use computers to increase profits?

Caregivers don't have much time left in the day to manage records. They're too busy spending time with clients. Computers can help by minimizing the time it takes to do the paperwork. Some caregivers utilize "soft time" (spent waiting during a client's nap, etc.) to keep records on a portable notebook computer.

Dating service

What will I be doing?

Are you a matchmaker at heart? Do you enjoy helping people find other people with similar interests? If so, consider operating a full- or part-time dating service from your home. A dating service is a personal introduction service for individuals of similar interests. You will be analyzing people's likes and dislikes, then helping them begin relationships with others of similar qualities. This really is a people business.

What will I need to start?

To be successful operating a dating service, you must first know something about people. You must know about personality types and what makes people the way they are. Even if you feel you already have these skills, get some training. Your customers will be counting on you to give them the best advice you can about other people. Knowledge is power.

Besides books and courses on human personality, you will also need an ability to organize information. In this computer age, there are programs that can help you gather and record information on people: contact software. You must develop an efficient system for matching people.

In addition, you will need a telephone for contacting people and allowing them to contact you.

Who will my customers be?

Customers for your dating service include individuals looking for companionship, marriage, or other relationships based on compatibility.

Many so-called dating services market themselves as introduction services. A few specialize in a specific type of client, especially services in areas of high competition for business. For example, a service may help vegetarians, nonsmokers, travelers, or those of a particular religion or ethnic group find matches. Once you've defined your customers by location or interests, finding them will be much easier.

How much should I charge?

How can you price your services? Of course so much depends on what services you offer and the time you must invest in offering them. Many dating services price based on an hourly rate of $35 to $50, but quoted as a specific fee. Some computer or video dating services charge initial membership fees of $1,000 or more—for a lifetime of dating leads. One successful introduction service charges $100 to $250 per introduction based on three to five hours of preparatory work. Many services charge about half the initial rate for introductions to additional people because much of the work of interviewing the client is already done.

How much will I make?

Your income as the owner of a dating service can vary. A small one-person office will typically have a gross income of $20,000 to $40,000 a year, limited by market size. Those who specialize and have a good reputation can earn $75,000 a year or more. Overhead expenses include your home office, computer, telephones, and advertising.

How can I get started?

One of the best ways of starting this or nearly any other business is to study your competitors. Become one of their clients, and you will learn what they are doing well and what could be improved— by you. Read the personal ads in local publications to learn who your potential competitors are, select the most successful for study, and contact them.

As you study your competitors, make notes on how you would improve on their services. In addition, spend some time learning about personality types and how to identify them. A large bookstore can help you find resources.

The SIC code for dating services is 7299-26.

How can I use computers to increase profits?

Computers are great tools for matchmakers. They can help you keep track of clients in a database, then quickly search the database for interests, personal traits, and other information to make the best match. Databases can also help you be more accurate in matches by keeping track of successes, failures, and the reasons for both.

Personal fitness trainer

What will I be doing?

The fitness craze has been around for some time, but there seems to be renewed interest. If you're into fitness and want to help others in their training, consider becoming a personal fitness trainer. A personal fitness trainer helps clients set and achieve personal fitness goals. Most fitness trainers specialize in exercise but also help with diet and even with breaking bad habits.

What will I need to start?

To train others in physical fitness, you must be a good example of the results. That doesn't mean you have to look like a body builder or a professional wrestler, but you do have to look and be healthy. You are your best advertisement.

To start, learn as much as you can about the why and how of physical fitness. Read the latest books and magazines. Find out what works best. Take some courses from a college extension or at a fitness center. Most important, learn how to motivate others toward good fitness habits.

You may work with people in your home, their home, or in a gymnasium. Take your choice. Many personal fitness trainers meet clients at a local gym. One trainer works with a group of six that meets in one section of a local gym on Saturday mornings. Another trainer visits homes where customers have exercise equipment, coaching and encouraging them.

Who will my customers be?

Your customers will usually be individuals who want to look and feel better. You can find them through advertisement in local newspapers, on gym bulletin boards, and by circulating your brochure.

Sometimes you can contract with a company to help employees meet physical fitness goals individually and as a group. One company offered to donate $5 to charity for every pound an employee lost during a specific month, hiring a personal fitness trainer to help and track results.

How much should I charge?

Many personal fitness trainers establish an hourly rate of $35 to $75. Newer trainers may establish lower rates for the first six months, until they establish a following. Trainers then may price services by the length and number of sessions or by the goal.

How much will I make?

About 20 percent of your time will be required to market your services, depending on your marketing skills, your credentials, and your customers. Plan to spend more time marketing as you start your business. Overhead will range from 10 to 40 percent depending on whether you furnish equipment, rent a room, or have other costs. Some trainers need an office while others have prospects contact them through a gym.

How can I get started?

Contact gyms, dance studios, and other commercial fitness businesses in your area to discuss your credentials and ideas. If you don't yet have credentials, join the American Fitness Association or a similar professional group and develop credentials.

Produce a flyer that includes your credentials, your programs, your prices, and information on how to contact you. Give these brochures away anywhere and everywhere.

How can I use computers to increase profits?

Physical fitness is important to you and your customers. Good recordkeeping is, too. You will want to schedule sessions, maintain up-to-date client files, track client progress toward goals, and, of course, track your income and expenses. Computers can do all these tasks and more. Start with an office suite (word processor, database manager, spreadsheet) and add a checking or accounting program.

Placement service

What will I be doing?

There are more than 18,000 placement agencies in the United States. Some are located in professional office buildings, but a growing number of them are operated from home offices. Some never see their clients, working exclusively by telephone and fax machine.

A placement service works with individuals looking for jobs as well as businesses seeking candidates for job openings. Your job will be to assist clients in identifying, approaching, and securing a satisfying job or candidate for a job. It's a rewarding business for both the owner and the clients. It requires extensive skills and experience, but can bring the owner an excellent income for an enjoyable task.

What will I need to start?

To help people find the job best suited to them, the placement counselor must have extensive experience in hiring, managing, and placing employees. This experience must be based on professional skills that take years to develop. In addition, a placement counselor must have access to a variety of testing and human resource tools and materials and have a familiarity with the local job market.

Who will my customers be?

There is certainly no shortage of potential customers who will benefit from qualified placement services. They include unemployed and underemployed individuals as well as companies who need help placing or replacing current employees.

Customers will find you through ads and by professional referral. So it will be important for you to make ties with the employment community in your area. Up to half of your customers will be referrals.

How much should I charge?

The rate placement services use to calculate their pricing is $40 to $80 an hour. However, most placement services quote prices calculated on a commission based on the value of a new job. Depending on what services are offered and how much of your time it takes for the typical placement, you may price your services at one-month's salary or even 25 percent of the annual salary of your client's new job.

How much will I make?

Because your business is operated from your home, overhead expenses are lower than if you had to rent a plush office downtown. In fact, overhead expenses including telephone, advertising, supplies, and related expenses will range from 20 to 35 percent of gross income. Deduct typical taxes and you'll probably get to keep about 50 cents to 60 cents of every dollar you charge clients. Collecting your fees can be more difficult in this business than in others, so learn how to reduce overdue receivables.

How can I get started?

This is one profession where credentials are more valuable than in others. People want more than your word that you are qualified to help them find the right job. If you have extensive experience in employment, make sure your prospects know it. Join professional associations, especially those that offer certification programs. Join local professional groups that add credibility to your business. Work hard to earn referrals.

The SIC code for placement services is 7361-03.

How can I use computers to increase profits?

Jobs are won and lost on the Internet. You can log on to the Internet and check the large job placement boards (like *www.monster.com*), view jobs offered through your state's department of employment (such as *www.caljobs.ca.gov*), and search hundreds of other resources. In addition, you can accept and submit resumes electronically via e-mail as well as correspond with clients. Computers are powerful tools for placement services.

Referral service

What will I be doing?

If you've ever needed help finding someone to perform a service, you know how handy it would be to have a single source to call—a referral service.

If you're one of those people that others call for referrals, you may be able to offer your networking knowledge to others for money without leaving home. You can start your own referral service.

A referral service finds, qualifies, selects, and promotes businesses that meet a specific business criteria or ethic. A referral service recommends and refers potential customers to businesses and associations for various services.

Some examples of successful referral services can include home repair, auto repair, medical or dental services, spiritual centers, and restaurants, to name a few.

What will I need to start?

A referral service is paid for knowledge of resources. The more knowledge and resources you have and the more valuable they are to your customers, the more you will be paid.

Referral services typically specialize in the needs of a specific group of customers. One may offer industrial contacts to foreign

buyers. Another referral service may check out and refer travel services to corporate customers. A third service will help new people in
a community find qualified doctors, dentists, attorneys, real estate
offices ,and other professional service. You'll most likely choose a
specialty that matches your own background and experience, or in
an area that is of special interest to you.

Who will my customers be?

Your customers are a group of people that need specific services.
They may be defined by their industry, their job, or where they live.
They all need information they don't have time to gather. They need
someone trustworthy to help them find other trustworthy people and
resources, and that is where your services will be essential.

Once you've decided who your customers are, finding them will
be much easier. A service ad in a local newspaper can promote your
handyman referral service. A brochure to restaurants can promote
your service of finding and referring the best restaurant suppliers.

How much should I charge?

The hourly rate for referral services ranges from $25 to $50. Your
pricing will be based on the time required to develop your referrals,
but more on the value of these referrals to your customers. If your
customers will save thousands of dollars by using your referrals, charging a few hundred dollars will be reasonable. If you're simply referring a plumber to a homeowner, your fee will be less because the
value is less. In some cases, the fee is paid for by the resource.

How much will I make?

Contacts will be everything in this business. Once you've developed qualified contacts in your field, most of your time will be spent
on offering these resources to customers. About 20 percent of your
time will be needed for promoting your services.

Expenses for a home-based referral service are typically 20 to 40
percent of income. This covers your office expenses, telephone, and
taxes. As your home-based business grows, you can focus your attention on customers and services that bring you the greatest profits
and satisfaction.

How can I get started?

To start a referral service, pick a service and a group of customers you enjoy working with and who need your skills. Then talk to
people in this group to learn what they need and how you can help.

Ask them what a good referral is worth to them. Remember to ask your resources if they would pay a finder's fee for your referrals.

Finally, start small, help a customer or two and learn. When you've defined your market and services, produce a flyer that you can circulate to potential customers.

How can I use computers to increase profits?

Knowledge is power. This is especially true to those who make money referring people for a fee. The more you know, the more you can make. Computers and the Internet offer a vast world of knowledge to help you match needs and resources. Learn to use the Internet as a research tool as well as a communications tool to keep in touch with clients and resources.

Reunion planner

What will I be doing?

Everybody is curious about the whereabouts of their high school or college classmates. What are they doing now? What ever happened to so-and-so? Did our class president ever get out of prison? It's this curiosity that drives people to slim down, get a tan, and attend their class reunion. If you enjoy reunions or at least enjoy organizing social events, consider planning reunions from your home.

What will I need to start?

Planning a reunion requires organizational skills, some research skills, a few selling skills, and a love for putting on a party. The best way to start a reunion-planning service is to volunteer to put one on for a group to which you belong. It can be a high school, college or trade school class, a military unit, a historical church, or any other institution that draws people together. It can even be a reunion of employees lost in the big layoff of 10 years ago.

If you have a computer, you'll need a database program for developing an address book of people to reunite. Otherwise, use file cards. You'll also need people skills as well as some event-planning skills for finding a meeting place and hiring caterers and entertainment.

Who will my customers be?

Your customers will be individuals who are or have belonged to a group, whether a school, class, church, military group, company or family, and may want to renew friendships with others in the group.

How will you find your customers? Once you've identified the type of reunions you will specialize in planning, contact the organizations to learn what, if any, plans have been made for reunions. For example, call area high schools asking if any class reunions are being planned and, if so, who is coordinating them. If not, ask how you could contact members to plan reunions.

How much should I charge?

It's difficult to set an hourly rate for reunion planning because much of the work is detail. If you can standardize or automate your methods for efficiency, you can establish a rate of $30 to $60 an hour. Who pays? Each attendee will pay a cover charge for attending the event. You may also get a fee from suppliers such as caterers, hotels, or others that benefit from your event.

How much will I make?

A class reunion of 200 people, each paying a $25 cover charge, can bring you an income of $5,000. You will have catering or other expenses to pay from this, but your net income should be at least half of this amount. The cover charge will be smaller if your meeting is at a restaurant where people will order their own food off the menu.

Your overhead costs will go for research, telephone calls, advertising, mailings, and taxes.

How can I get started?

The best way to learn this specialized business is to volunteer to put on a class reunion. Next, tackle reunions for local high schools, especially those where you or your children or friends have gone as you will have contacts. Some schools will rent you a meeting place for the reunion while others won't.

How can I use computers to increase profits?

The Internet can help you find and reunite people from around the world whether they are classmates, first loves, co-workers, or even enemies. Online you can search telephone books, public records, and other resources. To learn more about how the Internet has linked classmates, take a look at *www.classmates.com*.

Route sales

What will I be doing?

Route sales is a home-based business that requires a lot of travel. The typical route salesperson may spend 30 or more hours a week on the road traveling from customer to customer.

So what does a route sales business do? It sells products to retailers in a specific territory. An example is a person who sells and delivers candy to convenience stores or laundry to motels along a specific route.

What will I need to start?

To sell a product you must know about it and about competitive products. If you have a candy route you must know varieties, wholesale and retail pricing, packaging, displays, and how to best promote your product. You will also need to know who your competitors are and how your product compares in many areas.

You must also know how to be courteous and helpful. In many cases, products are sold by relationships as well as value. Give good, honest service and your products will sell better and you will profit more. You will probably need a delivery vehicle or at least a car in which you travel your route and take orders for later delivery.

Who will my customers be?

Customers for your route sales business include retailers or service businesses. You will be selling on behalf of wholesalers or manufacturers. You are not an employee but an independent contractor. In most cases you will buy the merchandise and wholesale it to the retailers.

How much should I charge?

Route salespeople are paid by commission on sales and sometimes reimbursed for sales expenses (truck, warehouse, etc.). A candy route salesperson will buy candy from a wholesaler or manufacturer and resell it to retail stores. Your prices will be dictated by the wholesaler or manufacturer and market conditions.

How much will I make?

A route salesperson will spend about 25 percent of gross income on overhead expenses, about 50 percent on the product, and keep the other 25 percent as net income (before taxes). Using this ratio, selling $3,000 in merchandise each week will net you about $750 a week or $39,000 a year. Again, much depends on what you sell, how you sell, to whom you sell, how competitive the market is, and other factors. Your profits will grow with the experience you gain.

How can I get started?

First, you must be a salesperson. A good salesperson can sell nearly any product. So learn the basics of selling and get some experience in the field to increase your chances of success.

Second, you need a product line. Interview potential customers to find products that offer an opportunity for you. Stay away from selling elephants and bridges as they are too difficult to deliver. Select products that you can deliver as you sell them, reducing transportation costs. Check area telephone books for wholesalers of your product line.

Third, make friends. In an age when retailers order from catalogs and by telephone, a friendly face can get an order—as long as the salesperson is helpful and patient.

How can I use computers to increase profits?

Route sales means recordkeeping. Who ordered what? When do they need it? How much did they pay? Will I make any money on the sale? Did I forget to include some expense and cut into my profit? Portable computers, called "notebooks" become the route salesperson's order book, order tracker, and recordkeeper. You can make your own order book using a standard database program or you can find one tailored to route sales. Talk with other route sales people about the software tools that work for them.

Sales representative

What will I be doing?

If you enjoy selling, but don't want to buy or deliver products for resale, consider becoming a sales representative. Believe it or not, this is one of the most popular home-based businesses in the United States—more people choose this as a home-based business than any other.

A sales representative helps bring buyers and sellers together on behalf of the seller, typically a manufacturer or wholesaler. This can be done in person or by phone. A sales representative for a business computer software company, for example, may make initial contact with a prospect by mail and phone, then set an appointment to demonstrate the system at the prospect's place of business. Another sales rep may never see customers face-to-face, working exclusively by telephone and mail with products shipped directly from the factory.

What will I need to start?

What could you sell to others? If you have experience in manufacturing or with a specific product, you could turn your knowledge into profits as a sales representative for a previous employer or even a competitor.

What contacts do you have? If you know lots of people in a specific field—dentists, accountants, car dealers, professional bowlers—you can find products and services that they need and help them buy.

So, you need both products and contacts. Of course, you also need selling skills that you can get with training or experience.

Who will my customers be?

Your customers will be manufacturers, wholesalers, retailers, or consumers. Most sales representatives are actually manufacturers' representatives, selling related products from a specific manufacturer. Others sell a variety of products handled by one or two wholesalers. Of course, your customers will also be those to whom you sell: retailers or consumers.

How much should I charge?

Sales reps get paid a commission that ranges from 2 percent for large-ticket (expensive) items to 35 percent or more for intangibles like radio advertising. So you won't usually set the price of what you sell. It will be set for you by your client.

How much will I make?

A lazy sales rep will soon go broke. A knowledgeable and energetic sales rep can make a comfortable living of $50,000 or more a year. If you find the right product and company to work with, that number can go even higher. Because you don't have to handle inventory, expenses are as low as 15 to 25 percent of your commissions.

How can I get started?

Learn how to sell. Take courses and read books on salesmanship. Be an expert on the products you plan to sell. Find qualified prospects and learn why and how they buy. Promote your business. Keep good records. Give better-than-average service.

Find manufacturers in the *Thomas Register of Manufacturers*, a multi-volume directory found at larger libraries.

Contact the Manufacturers' Agents National Association (714-859-4040) for more information.

How can I use computers to increase profits?

Salespeople are typically paid a commission on what they sell. No sales, no money. That's why you need to make sure you keep track of exactly what you sell, for how much, and your margin. You must also track business expenses that can lower your tax obligation.

Sales software packages are available that can make the task easier. Read sales trade journals for ads that offer sales software.

Seminar service

What will I be doing?

People profit from learning. If you have knowledge that others can profit from, consider offering a seminar service. If not, produce seminars that employ experts.

A seminar service designs, produces, coordinates, and markets seminars on specific topics of value to others. If your expertise is in childcare, for example, produce a short seminar for parents or those who work in the profession. Or hire an expert to teach in a seminar you produce.

There are many good opportunities to teach and to earn an attractive income with a seminar service.

What will I need to start?

To start a seminar service you first need to have some knowledge to offer—then you need to identify a group who will benefit from that knowledge. It may be in a field where you are an expert or it may be one in which you have an interest. You will then organize the information for use by others and present it to them in a way that helps them retain it.

You will also need a meeting place. Some cities have popular seminar meeting sites either in a convention center or at a popular hotel. Others hold seminars at schools or colleges. You'll need to identify and learn about renting such a site.

You will also need to reach potential customers of your seminars. This may be through newspaper advertisements and publicity or by contacting local business associations.

Who will my customers be?

Your customers will be those who will benefit from what you have to teach. In many cases, the greatest benefits are to those who financially profit from your knowledge, such as businesses or investors. They can make money with knowledge so they will pay more for that knowledge than someone who only gets pleasure from your knowledge.

A professional writer may offer a seminar to would-be writers. A security consultant can offer seminars on improving home security or on alarm installation. An experienced truck driver may offer a seminar on how to drive to stay alive. Define your topic and your best customers.

How much should I charge?

Seminar fees are $35 to $80 an hour, priced by the value of the seminar, time, and competition. Of course, the cost is split among all attendees. For example, a seminar that requires 16 hours of preparation and four hours of teaching at $40 an hour has a cost of $800. If split among 50 attendees, the price per attendee is $16. Add snacks and beverage service, room rental, and a factor for no-shows, and your seminar fee may be $30 per person.

How much will I make?

Most of your time will be billable to one seminar or another. Overhead costs range from 15 to 45 percent depending on whether you're including travel expenses and need expensive advertising.

Some seminars reduce costs by negotiating a percentage rental fee for the meeting site. A hotel may agree to free rental of a conference room in exchange for 10 percent of the seminar fees collected. Another may offer the room free if the seminar brings in 10 or more overnight guests.

Your actual income from this venture depends so much on your ability to organize and market. The range is $25,000 to $100,000 a year, but it can go even higher once you've developed your reputation as the producer of valuable seminars.

How can I get started?

The first step to starting a successful seminar service is to learn from the successes of others. If you haven't already done so, attend various seminars in your area. Study how the seminar is organized and conducted. Calculate estimated costs and income from fees to estimate whether it is profitable. Decide how you would do it better.

Then try organizing your own seminar through local community colleges or adult education resources. The administrator may help you plan and market the seminar. Keep lots of notes. Learn from failures. Do better.

How can I use computers to increase profits?

Seminars are typically promoted with mailers or brochures sent to a specific group of potential attendees. Computer software and the Internet can help you design and write the mailer, find valuable mailing lists, and even print the address labels for the mailers. In addition, you can promote your seminars using your own Web page.

Senior day-care center

What will I be doing?

For many, retirement is a time to travel, fish, or otherwise do all the things that couldn't be done while earning a living and raising a family. Yet there are many seniors, particularly those who are older or infirm, who may not be as independent as they once were, but still want a place to go on a regular basis.

You can help these people by offering a day-care center for seniors. Some of the seniors may live on their own while others live with family members. Perhaps they feel more comfortable with some contact during the day when family members aren't home. Or perhaps they just want the companionship of other senior adults. You can provide a place for such people. If you have an area in your home that could be used for social gatherings, TV-watching, meals, and some recreation such as cards or games, you might have what it takes to start a senior day-care center.

What does a senior day-care center do? It offers limited care, meals, and activities to seniors during daytime hours at your home. Their children may drop the seniors off on the way to work, or they may come in on their own.

What will I need to start?

Of course, you need a location where seniors can feel comfortable and get good care. An unused family room with an outside entrance is perfect, but even a living room and dining room can be used for this business. Make sure you aren't breaking any zoning laws. Eventually you may decide to convert a garage into your senior center.

You'll either need a place to prepare meals or to serve meals prepared elsewhere. You'll need to have access for those with limitations or disabilities. You'll need activities besides the television. You may even need a passenger van for taking seniors shopping or to appointments.

Who will my customers be?

Users of your senior day-care center will, of course, be older adults. In some cases they will also be your customers or clients who pay you for care. Otherwise you will be paid by the children of seniors or by social service agencies. You may need licensing or certification. Contact your regional Small Business Administration to find out what requirements your business must meet.

How much should I charge?

Your charge for caring for seniors placed by state agencies will be defined and paid by the agency. If you are offering care services to individuals, you will set your own price based on costs of the services you provide and the number of seniors you care for. Some care centers start with a day rate of $15 to $20 including a meal and snacks. Others base their pricing on how much state agencies will pay and look to the senior or the family to provide the balance, if any. You will also charge by time as some seniors will only be with you a portion of the day or week while others may get care in excess of 40 hours a week.

How much will I make?

This is an especially good business if you already have one or two senior parents living in your home. It offers them companionship and you an income from your other clients. But don't expect to get rich from this business. The typical senior day-care center with six or less seniors under full-time care will net the business owner under $20,000 a year after expenses.

How can I get started?

Giving care to seniors requires skill and patience. If you feel you have those qualifications, first volunteer to work with seniors so you can develop experience and resources. Next, start looking at your home and how you can provide for seniors there. Then contact local social services and zoning offices to learn what requirements such a business will have. Some communities are friendlier to home-based service businesses than others.

Once you're ready, start advertising your services in local senior papers and through your contacts.

How can I use computers to increase profits?

How can you expense your television, furniture, and home for your senior day-care business? What legitimate expenses can you deduct from your tax obligation? These and other questions can be answered online by the Internal Revenue Service at *www.irs.gov.*

Show promoter

What will I be doing?

If you enjoy promoting events, consider doing it for money from your home. A show promoter designs, coordinates, funds, and markets events and shows for specific groups. You might bring a rock-and-roll revival show to town, or you may produce a local car show. Do what you love. This work involves a lot of organizing, making phone calls, and developing contacts and connections. In some ways this line of work can be said to require the skills of an event planner with the connections of a talent agent.

What will I need to start?

You must have proven experience in promotion: Maybe you've helped a local civic group put on a talent show or a special fund-raising event or maybe you've helped coordinate the arrival of an out-of-town speaker for your church. You have a real desire to learn more about show promotion.

To promote a show you will need to know who else promotes events in your area as well as what media (radio, TV, newspapers) are typically used. You will also need to have contacts within your field such as national booking agents.

Who will my customers be?

Your customers will be those who pay admission or a fee to bring an entertainer or speaker to your area. You may organize a local program for a touring musical group or a prominent personality, but your ultimate customers will be those who pay the bills.

You can find your customers by first identifying what types of shows you want to promote: business, entertainment, education, religious, etc. Then finding and contacting customers will be much easier. If your business tries to be all things to all people, it will probably serve none of them well enough to be profitable.

How much should I charge?

Show or event promoters earn a good income with rates of $35 to $75 an hour. Most are paid by percentage of gate receipts or profits, or a set fee based on estimated time required to produce. For example, a promoter who produces a one-day seminar of business speakers may earn 10 percent of the admission fees plus 5 to 10 percent of the back-of-the-room sales of books and videos. A music show promoter's percent of gate receipts will probably be larger, but so will the risk of loss.

How much will I make?

Show promoters will build their business to a specific number of events per year or season. A music promoter may try to produce three or four shows during the summer or six during the year. A seminar promoter may work on just one or two sessions per year. Income from these events will range from $25,000 to $75,000 a year after talent fees and overhead costs are paid.

How can I get started?

Show promotion is a craft. It requires attention to detail, promotional skills, a knowledge of the entertainment industry, contacts within the field being promoted and an understanding of what shows will do best in the area. Gain these skills and you'll have laid the foundation for potential success as a show promoter.

How can I use computers to increase profits?

Modern show promoters do much of their work on computers. They check artists' and booking agents' Web sites for availability, e-mailing offers and agreements. They book the venue online. They promote the event online. And they produce fliers promoting the event using desktop publishing software. See Chapter 3 for even more ideas.

Telephone answering service

What will I be doing?

Many people hate answering machines. Some hang up. Others leave cryptic messages. Opportunity! If you have experience answering telephone inquiries or taking and relaying messages for people, you can turn this opportunity into a home business. You can start a telephone answering service.

What will I need to start?

Besides one or more telephone lines, there are few things you need to start your own successful telephone answering service. You will want a call-record system and some information sheets from clients. You'll also want a smiling voice for greeting callers.

Who will my customers be?

Most of your customers will be professional people who may also have home-based businesses. A manufacturer's representative, an appliance repair service, a rental manager, and others may be your clients. For them you will either handle all calls or only those that come in while they are unavailable.

A successful service is owned by a woman with young children. She takes referral calls from area businesses after they close up for the day. Most of her calls come in between 8 p.m. and 2 a.m. and on weekends. She logs the calls and, early the next morning, faxes the logs to the appropriate businesses.

How much should I charge?

Telephone answering services establish a per-hour rate with a charge for more calls than are typical. For example, the rate may be $2 an hour or $8 for a four-hour shift plus 25¢ per call over 10 in an hour. Pricing is based on the expected length of the typical call. If most calls will require less than one minute of your time, pricing will be lower than if you must relay lengthy messages or answer a number of questions.

In most cases you will also charge a setup fee for new clients to cover costs of adding or changing telephone lines plus training.

How much will I make?

Overhead expenses for your telephone answering service will be 10 to 35 percent of income. Long-distance charges will be additional. A telephone answering service can earn the owner $20,000 to $30,000 a year depending on services offered and marketing abilities. For 24-hour service, some answering services contract with other home-based operators to make sure all hours are covered.

How can I get started?

First, check the local telephone book for answering services advertised. Who are they? What exchanges do they cover? What services do they offer? Call them to learn their rates and setup fees.

Next, start planning your own telephone answering service. Learn the cost and requirements of bringing additional lines into your home.

Finally, start asking your friends and acquaintances for opportunities. You may answer after-hour calls for your doctor, lawyer, dentist, or accountant—or for friends who are professionals. Place a small ad in the service directory of your local newspaper, especially in the business section. Let people know what you do and how to contact you.

The SIC code for telephone answering services is 7389-03.

How can I use computers to increase profits?

Telephone answering services use computers to track clients, income, expenses, and schedules. In addition, computers can become fax machines for automatically sending and receiving information.

Telephone survey service

What will I be doing?

It's the call that everyone hates: the telephone survey at dinner time. But the people on the other end of the telephone provide a valuable service and can do so with friendliness and sensitivity.

They can also make money from home.

If you'd like to bring your energy and enthusiasm to a business that sorely needs it, consider operating a telephone survey service. Find an approach that encourages trust and conversation. Treat each caller like a person and your exceptional results will profit you in many ways.

What will I need to start?

To conduct telephone surveys you must know how to graciously get information from other people. You need to know how to politely probe. You may follow a prewritten script. If allowed, you may be able to vary how you ask a question for improved results.

Of course, you'll also need a telephone and an answering system if you expect return calls. Also consider investing in a head set (about $100) to prevent tired arms and neck.

Depending on what type of surveying you do, you may need a computer and related software. One successful telephone survey service conducts post-travel interviews for a tour company, asking how the customer enjoyed the trip and what could be improved. She works at a computer that handles all dialing and gives her a place to write the responses. Once a day, her reports are electronically mailed to her supervisor in another city.

Who will my customers be?

Customers for your home-based telephone survey service include small companies that market to individuals or other companies.

Businesses want to know who will buy certain things or what they have bought. You can specialize in inquiry follow-up or did-you-buy calls that are placed a month after people request information about your customer's product or service. Or you may specialize in market research surveys that try to learn what people want from specific products.

Your customers will be businesses, advertising agencies, inquiry management services, fund-raising organizations, and others who need to know what their prospects or customers are thinking.

How much should I charge?

The rate for telephone survey varies from $30 to $75 an hour, priced by value of information, the call, or other measurable variables. One service charges by the number of responses gained in surveys. Another charges per call, whether the person completes the survey or not.

How much will I make?

Most of your time at this job will be billable to a client and overhead expenses are low. If you are good at your job, you can make a net income of $12 to $25 an hour after expenses. The more valuable the information you gather is to someone, the more you will be paid.

How can I get started?

Some people start this business by working for a phone shop, a business that has dozens of people making telemarketing calls from a big room. Unfortunately, it is easy to pick up bad habits, such as speaking to a telephone rather than a person and watching the clock. You may get better training by teaching yourself the needed skills at your own pace. Volunteer to make survey calls for the American Red Cross or another well-respected group. You'll learn as much without the pressure.

Once your experience is developed, contact local businesses to tell them what you can do for them: You can call their customers and prospects to get valuable information that will help the business grow and profit. Few businesses can afford to turn down a conversation with customers.

How can I use computers to increase profits?

Today's telephone survey takers use computers to maintain calling scripts, enter survey results, and even dial telephone numbers for them from a list. Database programs are useful for tracking and charting responses. You can easily make reports and e-mail them to your clients.

Temporary help agency

What will I be doing?

One of the best ways of developing skills for your home business is to hire yourself out as a temporary worker in your chosen field. You will quickly get on-the-job training without the obligations of a long-term job. You may also meet some of your prospective customers.

You may also decide to operate your own home-based temporary help agency. Such a service finds temporary laborers, office workers, salespeople, and even professionals for business, industry, and individuals. In many areas, temporary help agencies specialize in domestic, day-labor, crafts, office, or other workers.

What will I need to start?

There are nearly 18,000 temporary help agencies in the United States. Competition for quantity is high, but competition for quality is never very high—so offer quality service.

To start your temporary help service you will, obviously, need some temporary help. You will need to match jobs with qualified workers. In most cases, you'll gather workers through your advertisements and jobs through ads and outbound calls to employers. So you'll need a telephone and a card file or computer system to track all your resources.

Who will my customers be?

Your customers will be retail businesses, manufacturers, service businesses, and individuals who have a job to be done but don't want to hire a full-time person to do it. To minimize bookkeeping, the employers prefer to pay a fee to a temporary help service who will find qualified workers, make sure they are at the job, and take care of pay and taxes.

Who hires temporary help? Offices need a replacement for a vacationing secretary. A warehouse needs workers to help unload a big shipment coming in tomorrow morning. A homeowner needs a temporary domestic helper for the holidays.

How much should I charge?

Temporary help services usually hire the employees directly as needed, paying taxes and sometimes benefits, collecting a higher fee from the employer. For example, a laborer may be hired by the service for $8 an hour to unload trucks for a couple of days. The agency may get $16 an hour for the laborer's time, passing on half of it to the laborer and keeping the rest. After expenses, the agency may get a quarter of the fee, or about $4 an hour. To make money, the agency must have many workers out on jobs at any given time.

How much will I make?

You can make a little or a lot, depending on how efficient you are at finding and matching jobs and workers. You can work late afternoons finding jobs and evenings finding workers for those jobs. A standard workday can give you a weekly income of $1,000 or more. Or not. If not, look for jobs or workers that are easier to find and coordinate.

Your overhead costs, excluding payroll and taxes, will range from 25 to 50 percent of your portion of the pay. If you have five workers out at $12 an hour each and you pay them $6 an hour each, you're making $30 an hour. Your overhead will take up a quarter to a half of your portion after taxes are paid.

How can I get started?

Many temporary help services are started by those who have experience as temporary workers. They know how the local market works, who needs temps, and where to find them. They also know the importance of good service. If you don't have experience as a temp, become one for a while to learn the business from the other side.

Once you're ready to go into business for yourself, select a field of labor, contact temp employers, and start lining up temporary employees. Develop business cards and fliers to help you promote your business.

For more information contact the National Association of Temporary Services (703-549-6287).

The SIC code for temporary help agencies is 7363-04.

How can I use computers to increase profits?

Temp services must keep accurate and up-to-date records of employers and employees, jobs, taxes, expenses, and many other facts. That's where computers shine. They are math machines that follow instructions from software and users. Database software can manage many of these tasks, with files for temps, potential employers, and related data. Checking software can help track income and expenses. Payroll software can help take care of that headache.

Tutoring service

What will I be doing?

People want to learn. Learning may not always be enjoyable, but it is often necessary. If you are knowledgeable on a topic, you can make it more enjoyable—or at least easier—for others to learn. You can be a tutor. Alternately, you can help people find qualified tutors.

As a tutor you will help others learn facts or skills about a subject in which you are proficient. Tutors help students learn remedial or advanced topics.

What will I need to start?

To teach a subject you must first have extensive knowledge on the topic. You don't necessarily have to be an expert, but you must at least know more than the student. You must also know how to transfer that knowledge to your student. Practical experience with the topic may be all that's needed to make the subject come alive. For example, in teaching physics, conducting experiments can help the student visualize concepts and learn faster than reading from the book. So, depending on your subject, you may need lab equipment.

In some states, tutors must be certified and licensed. Check with area colleges on requirements for tutors in your state.

Who will my customers be?

In most cases your customers will be the parents of high school students, or college students themselves. You can reach the parents or students through advertising and brochures. They may also be adults who are going back to school. Referrals from teachers are very useful.

How much should I charge?

Your hourly rate as a tutor will depend on the topic, complexity of the material, your credentials, and your teaching skills. As a successful tutor you will be able to establish a higher rate than new tutors. Typical rates are $25 to $50 an hour with most tutors on the lower end of the scale—unless the subject is graduate-level quantum physics.

Some tutorial services offer a package deal like this: On-call tutoring is offered as needed and priced by course. For example, a chemistry tutor will help a student throughout the course whenever a question arises or to prepare for an upcoming test for a flat fee of $200 per course. One tutor located in the Midwest has a toll-free number for students and charges services by the hour to their credit card.

How much will I make?

About 80 percent of your time will be billable once your business is established. Overhead expenses for reference materials, telephone, office supplies, and some advertising will range from 20 to 40 percent. So a tutor working 30 billable hours a week at $25 an hour with 20 percent overhead will net $600 a week, or more than $30,000 a year.

How can I get started?

If you have little or no experience as a tutor, develop your skills by volunteering to tutor others on your primary subjects. Develop your resources. If one or two textbooks are most popular in your field, buy them or ask for them from students whom you're done tutoring.

Ask for referrals. If you're in college, ask teachers and professors if they would recommend you to lower division students. Also ask your students for referrals. Produce a flyer on your skills and include your telephone number or another way to contact you. Include references or testimonials.

The SIC code for tutors and tutoring services is 8299-09.

How can I use computers to increase profits?

Many tutors use computers to develop lesson plans, correspond with students, research information on the Internet, schedule tutoring sessions, and track income and expenses. Using the Internet, you can help students anywhere in the world from your own home.

Wedding planner

What will I be doing?

The United States has more than 8,500 full-time wedding consultants, many working from their home. Would you like to join them? A wedding planner or consultant plans, budgets, arranges, and coordinates weddings and related events. A wedding planner helps take the stress out of an emotional event.

What will I need to start?

To be a wedding planner you must first be efficient. You must be able to coordinate many tasks at once, handling both people and situations with confidence and skill. Experience as a meeting or event planner will be helpful.

The greatest tool in a wedding planner's business is his or her notebook—or computer file. It holds the names of and data on prospects, clients, wedding resources, and other information for planning a successful wedding event. So you'll need to start collecting information on local wedding resources soon.

Who will my customers be?

Your customers are obvious: engaged couples and their relatives. What may not be as obvious is how to reach these potential customers. Local bridal fairs are a good source of leads if you can buy a list of the attendees or, better, have a booth there. Also develop friendships with wedding suppliers who can refer your services: photographers, churches, flower shops, cake decorators, etc.

How much should I charge?

Your hourly rate as a wedding planner will be $25 to $50. You will use this rate to establish a flat fee per event or a percentage of the wedding budget. Flat fees for planning a wedding range from $500 to $2,000 for the wedding event and reception. Or you can set your price as a percentage of the total event budget, typically 10 to 20 percent. Wedding suppliers (caterers, musicians, equipment rental) are paid separately.

How much will I make?

Your new wedding planning service will require as much as 30 percent of your time for marketing and promotion. Once established, about 10 percent of your time will probably be enough to keep your business moving at a profitable pace. Of course, this depends on your marketing skills, competition and referrals.

Overhead expenses for a wedding planner usually range from 15 to 30 percent after suppliers are paid. So a wedding that grosses $1,000 in income will net you $700 to $850 and probably require 15 to 25 hours to plan and manage.

How can I get started?

You may already have experience planning and coordinating wedding events. If not, start volunteering to do so for friends or relatives, asking for a letter of recommendation from them when the event is successfully done.

Contact the Association of Bridal Consultants (203-354-1404).

The SIC code for wedding consultants is 7299-32.

How can I use computers to increase profits?

What a beautiful wedding. It's the bridal consultant who should get the credit for much of the hard work that goes into a wedding. All in a day's work. Computers make the task easier by helping the bridal consultant keep track of all the details, contact and verify caterers and other services, track expenses and hours, and make sure everyone knows which church to be at on the wedding day. Computers should take a bow, too.

Part
3

Growing Your
Business

7 Where to Get Valuable Help

Most home businesses need a little help getting started. In fact, that's the purpose of this book: to help you start your own cottage company. This final chapter offers resources, ideas, tips, and suggestions from my small business consulting practice as well as from other successful home-business people.

Who will help you succeed—and why

Some of the valuable resources described here are services of the government. Benevolent? Not really. If your home business succeeds, the national economy improves—though maybe just slightly—and you pay more taxes. Your business may start in a home or in a garage (as did Hewlett-Packard and many others), someday expanding to a larger location and employing thousands of people.

Other resources offer to help because of the benefits they receive from your success. Suppliers, trade associations, bankers, and advertising firms all have a stake in your success. So they're willing to help you. Take advantage of this help—as long as there are few or no strings attached.

SBA: valuable help at little or no cost

Founded more than 40 years ago, the Small Business Administration (SBA) has offices in 100 cities across the United States and a charter to help small businesses start and grow. The SBA offers counseling and administers a small business loan guarantee program. To find your area's SBA office, check the white pages of metropolitan telephone books in your region under "United States Government, Small Business Administration." To contact the SBA, you can write to 1441 L Street NW, Washington, D.C. 20416, or call the Small Business Answer Desk at 800-827-5722. You can reach the SBA on the Internet at *www.sbaonline.sba.gov.*

The SBA also sponsors the 13,000 Service Corps of Retired Executives (SCORE) volunteers, Active Corps of Executives (ACE) volunteers, Business Development Centers, and Technology Access Centers.

The SBA offers numerous publications, services, and videos for starting and managing a small business. Publications are available on products, ideas, inventions, financial management, management and planning, marketing, crime prevention, personnel management, and other topics. The booklets can be purchased for $1 or $2 each at SBA offices or from SBA Publications, P.O. Box 30, Denver, CO 80201. Ask first for SBA Form 115A, *The Small Business Directory*, which lists available publications and includes an order form.

Another popular service is SBA On-Line, a computer bulletin board operated by the SBA. It receives more than 1,000 calls a day and has handled one million calls since it opened in 1992. If you're familiar with computers and modems, you can access this resource by having your system call 900-463-4636. There is a small fee for use, currently about $6 an hour. The bulletin board includes extensive resources for small businesses as well as access to other government agencies. If you want to access a limited version of this popular bulletin board, dial 800-697-4636. It doesn't have as many resources, but it's free.

If you're already traveling the Internet, SBA On-Line can also be accessed on the World Wide Web at *www.sbaonline.sba.gov.* For technical help or more information, call 202-205-6400.

A new SBA resource is the U.S. Business Adviser, an online clearinghouse located on the Internet at *www.business.gov.* You may also be able to reach this small business resource through your online service.

If you're interested in applying for an SBA guaranteed or direct loan, call your regional office of the Small Business Administration. Even better, ask for the name of an SBA-certified lender in your area. The SBA loan program, notorious for its paperwork requirements, can be expedited by a lender who knows how to work within the system. You'll get your loan faster. In fact, those bankers who have preferred-lender status can handle your SBA loan without the SBA even being involved.

Free business counseling

SBA's Service Corps of Retired Executives (SCORE) is a national nonprofit association with a goal of helping small business. SCORE members donate their time and experience to counsel individuals regarding small business matters. For more information on SCORE, write to them at 409 Third Street SW, Fourth Floor, Washington, D.C. 20024, or call 800-634-0245. Their Internet address is *www.score.org.*

The 700 Business Development Centers (BDCs) are regional centers funded by the SBA and managed in conjunction with regional colleges. A BDC offers free and confidential counseling for small business owners and managers, new businesses, home businesses, and individuals with questions concerning retail, service, wholesale, manufacturing, and farm businesses. BDCs sponsor seminars on various business topics, assist in developing business and marketing plans, inform entrepreneurs of employer requirements and teach cash flow budgeting and management. BDCs also gather information sources, assist in locating business resources, and make referrals.

Small Business Institutes (SBIs) are partnerships between the SBA and nearly 500 colleges offering counseling services to area businesses. SBIs conduct market research, develop business and marketing plans, and help small businesses work out manufacturing problems. Contact your regional SBA office to find out if a local college has such a program. You could get free or low-cost assistance from the college's business faculty and students.

Free help with taxes

The U.S. Treasury Department's Internal Revenue Service offers numerous Small Business Tax Education Program videos through its regional offices. Topics include depreciation, business use of your home, employment taxes, excise taxes, starting a business, sole proprietorships, partnerships, self-employed retirement plans, Sub-Chapter S corporations, and federal tax deposits.

If you're considering using a portion of your home as a business office, request *Business Use of Your Home* (Publication 587) from the Internal Revenue Service (Washington, D.C. 20224). It's free and will help you determine if your business qualifies for this option as well as how to take advantage of it to lower your taxes. If so, you will add *Form 8829, Expenses for Business Use of Your Home*, to the sheaf of forms you file with your *Form 1040* and *Schedule C.*

Depending on how much you use your business vehicle for personal use, you can either list all costs of operating the vehicle as an expense or you can deduct a standard mileage rate as an expense when you file income taxes. For more information, request *Business Use of a Car* (Publication 917) from the Internal Revenue Service. There's no charge for this publication.

What business expenses are deductible? There's a long list. The best answer is found in a free publication offered by the Internal Revenue Service, *Business Expenses* (Publication 535).

To find out more about your tax obligations, contact your regional IRS office (or call 800-829-3676) for the following publications:

$ *Tax Guide for Small Business* (Publication 334).

$ *Guide to Free Tax Services* (Publication 910).

$ *Your Federal Income Tax* (Publication 17).

$ *Employer's Tax Guide* (Circular E).

$ *Taxpayers Starting a Business* (Publication 583).

$ *Self-Employment Tax* (Publication 533).

$ *Retirement Plans for the Self-Employed* (Publication 560).

$ *Tax Withholding and Estimated Tax* (Publication 505).

$ *Business Use of Your Home* (Publication 587).

The first publication on this list, *Tax Guide for Small Business,* is the most important. Request it as soon as you begin planning your business. It describes business organization, assets, profits, net income, taxes, and tax forms in clear language. It also includes sample tax forms filled in to illustrate how they are completed. A new edition is published each January on the prior tax year including important changes in the federal tax laws. Your state may have a similar publication for filing state business taxes.

You can also download these forms (Adobe Acrobat PDF format) from *www.irs.gov.*

Codes for defining your business

I've already introduced you to SICs in the first two chapters of this book. Now let me reveal why the special code I included at the end of most of the business profiles is so important. The Standard Industrial Classification coding system, established by the government, is a system for categorizing and coding nearly all types of businesses into common groups while allowing some flexibility for new business types.

Who cares? *You* should. Your home business will probably fall into a specific SIC. Your banker will want to know the SIC code for your business. So will the SBA, the IRS (on your *Schedule C/Form 1040*), and others. Also, you can use your customers' SIC codes to select specific mailing lists of new customers. Pretty handy.

How do SICs work? Here's an example: One of the home businesses discussed in this book is an auto detailing service. The SIC code for this business is 7542-03. The first two digits—75—fall within the range between 70 and 89, meaning it is a service business. There are more businesses in the service sector than in any other, including retail. Specifically, 75 includes "Automotive Repair Services and Parts." Going further, 7542 is the category for car washes. The suffix 03 takes the category even further to cover automobile detail and clean-up service. If the suffix were 04, the business would be an automobile upholstery cleaning service. You get the picture.

What can you learn from these numbers? You can find them on the Internet from OSHA at *www.osha.gov/oshstats/sicser.html*. In addition, list brokers such as American Business Lists (800-555-5335) sell mailing lists for specific SIC codes. The names and addresses come from telephone books and survey calls to businesses across the nation. According to broker listings, there are 11,215 businesses in the United States that match the SIC code for auto detailing services. Further, there are 1,553 in California (no surprises here) and 41 in Rhode Island. If you're starting an auto detail service, this is the number of your established competitors. If your home business is selling to auto detailers, this can be a list of your potential customers. ABL is also available online at *www.infousa.com*.

There are two other coding systems that can help you find your customers and your competitors: zip codes and SMSA codes. You're familiar with postal zip codes that identify specific geographic locations by the number of the post office serving the area. The five-digit code divides the country into 10 large geographic areas identified by the first digit—0 to 9. The second and third digits are used to divide states. The fourth and fifth digits represent local areas. Four additional digits, SMSA codes, can be added to identify a specific address.

SMSA stands for Standard Metropolitan Statistical Area, also known as MSA, for Metropolitan Statistical Area. Designated by the

U.S. Census Bureau, these are areas with at least 100,000 people with strong economic and social ties to a central city. For example, the Portland-Vancouver MSA includes the cities of Portland and Vancouver as a single economic entity, though they are in neighboring states on two sides of a river. The MSA includes not only Portland and Vancouver, but their suburbs where people work and shop. This is useful information if your home business will be serving a specific geographic area.

You can learn more about SMSA and the census on the Internet at *www.census.gov.*

The value of good records

Why keep records? There are many reasons. For the individual just starting a home business, a good record-keeping system increases the chances of survival.

Even an established home business can enhance its chances of staying in business and increasing profits with a good record-keeping system.

Good accounting records decrease the chances of failure and increase the likelihood of remaining in business and making a profit. The following are some of the questions that good business records can answer:

$ How much business am I doing?

$ How much credit am I extending?

$ How are my collections?

$ What are my losses from credit sales?

$ Who owes me money?

$ Who is delinquent?

$ Should I continue extending credit to delinquent accounts?

$ How much cash do I have on hand?

$ How much cash do I have in the bank?

$ Does this amount agree with what records tell me I should have, or is there a shortage?

$ How much have I invested in supplies?

$ How often do I turn over my supplies inventory?

$ How much do I owe my suppliers and other creditors?

$ How much gross profit or margin did I earn?

$ What were my expenses?

$ How much net profit did I earn?

$ How much income tax will I owe?

$ Are my sales, expenses, profits, and capital showing improvements or did I do better last year?

$ How do I stand as compared with two periods ago?

$ Is my business's position about the same, improving, or deteriorating?

$ On what services am I making a profit, breaking even, or losing money?

$ Are the discounts I get from suppliers as great as those I give to my customers?

$ How do the financial facts of my home business compare with those of similar businesses?

Get the point? Your business requires a good record-keeping system to help you work smarter rather than harder.

Keeping accurate and up-to-date business records is, for many people, the most difficult and uninteresting aspect of operating a business. If this area of business management is one that you believe will be hard for you, plan *now* how you will handle it. Don't wait until tax time or until you're totally confused.

Take a course at a local community college, ask a volunteer SCORE representative or hire an accountant to advise you on setting up and maintaining your record-keeping system.

Your records will be used to prepare tax returns, make business decisions, and apply for loans. Set aside a special time each day to update your records. It will pay off in the long run with more deductions and fewer headaches.

A good record-keeping system should be:

$ Simple to use.

$ Easy to understand.

$ Reliable.

$ Accurate.

$ Consistent.

$ Timely.

Several published systems and software systems provide simplified records, usually in a single record book. These systems cover the primary records required for all businesses, but some are modified specifically for the home business. Check your local office supply store, your trade association, or trade journals for more information on specialized record books.

To keep track of everything, you should have the following records (sample forms included in the appendix of this book):

1. **Income Reporter:** gives you a place to write down the income you receive from your cottage company. Remember that income is cash received rather than sales made. It isn't income until you get the money in hand.

2. **Expense Reporter:** a tool for recording the costs of your business including office expenses, product costs, labor, and other expenses.

3. **Cash Flow Reporter:** a useful tool to help you track when money is expected to come in and when it's scheduled to go out. You don't want to borrow money to pay expenses just because you forgot to collect from a customer.

4. **Inventory Reporter:** used by businesses selling or re-selling a product. It includes columns for keeping track of how many units you have so you don't have to back-order or tell customers you don't have any left.

5. **Income and Expense Worksheet:** combines information from the Income Reporter, the Expense Reporter, and other resources to help you calculate whether your home business is making a profit or a loss.

Some businesses combine all of these records into a single report. In fact, there are many good one-write systems available that allow you to make a single entry for each transaction. You can also use computer software such as Quicken (*www.quicken.com*), QuickBooks (*www.quickbooks.com*), or Microsoft Money (*www.microsoft.com/money)* to track income and expenses in a checkbook format.

Promoting your business at little cost

You can choose from many effective ways to advertise your home business at little or no cost. Exactly which methods you use depend somewhat on your specialization.

Once you have your business cards printed, carry a stack of them with you wherever you go. Pass them out to anyone who may be or know a prospect. As you stop for lunch, put your business card on the restaurant's bulletin board. Do the same if you stop at a local market. All it costs is the price of a business card.

Many home businesses overlook one of the best sources of free advertising—publicity. As you start your business, write a short article or press release, and give copies to your local newspaper, radio stations, and other media. Include in it information about your business, such as owners, experience, affiliations, background, expertise, purpose of the business, location, target market, and contact name. If your market is across an industry rather than a geographic area, send this press release to magazines in that particular trade—these are called trade journals.

You can promote your business and get free advertising by offering to write a weekly newspaper column on your specialty in exchange for an ad in the paper.

If you're personable and would be comfortable doing so, offer to host a radio call-in talk show on your specialty or a related topic. Or you can become a regular guest on someone else's talk show. The publicity will make you a local celebrity as well as an authority on your specialty.

When should you seek free publicity?

$ When you start your home business.

$ When you're ready to celebrate a company anniversary.

$ When you hire a new employee.

$ When you change or add a location.

$ When you introduce a new product or service.

$ When you take on a partner or incorporate.

$ When an employee earns a promotion or special award.

$ When your business is mentioned in another media.

$ When a large contract is signed (if you have the customer's permission to publicize).

As you can see, starting and running a successful home business involves many requirements, not the least of which are hard work and tenacity. Armed with those and the right information, you will be up to the challenge. Best wishes on finding and succeeding with your best home business. God bless!

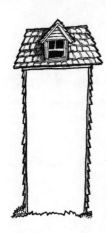

Appendix: Worksheets for Home Entrepreneurs

Opportunity Worksheet

What will I be doing?

To help you select and evaluate weekend home business opportunities in this book, first answer these questions:

What would I like to be doing (output)?

_____

_____

What would I need (inputs) to produce these outputs?

_____

_____

What business experience have I had?

_____

_____

What challenges or limitations do I have?

_____

_____

What time is or will soon be available to me?

    Daytime: _____

    Evenings: _____

    Weekends: _____

    Seasonal: _____

    Other: _____

What hours or days do I prefer to devote to a part-time business?

_____

_____

Resource Worksheet

What will I need to start?

To help you start weekend home business opportunities in this book, first answer these questions:

What knowledge or training do I have?

_____

_____

_____

What skills have I developed?

_____

_____

_____

What financial resources do I have?

_____

_____

_____

What tools and equipment do I have or can easily get?

_____

_____

_____

What other resources are available to me?

_____

_____

_____

Customer Worksheet

Who will my customers be?

To help you find customers for your weekend home business, answer these questions:

What products or services have I been a customer for?

_____

_____

_____

What have I learned about being a customer?

_____

_____

_____

What do I know about the needs of these potential customers?
    Individuals: _____
    Groups: _____
    Professionals: _____
    Retail businesses: _____
    Wholesalers: _____
    Manufacturers: _____
    Governments: _____
    Schools: _____

Where would I first look for customers?

_____

_____

What would be my motto or attitude toward my customers?

_____

_____

Price Analysis Worksheet

How much should I charge?

To help you price products and services for your weekend home business, answer these questions:

What hourly rate is typical for selected businesses?

_____

_____

What are the primary products and services I would offer?

_____

_____

How much time does each product or service require to produce?

_____

_____

What supplies or materials does each product or service require to produce?

_____

_____

What unit does each product or service use for pricing (session, job, page, etc.)?

_____

_____

How do my potential competitors price these products or services?

_____

_____

Income and Expense Worksheet

How much will I make?

To help you figure profits from your weekend home business, answer these questions:

What will my hourly rate probably be?

_____

_____

About how much of my business time will be billable?

_____

_____

What and how much will my overhead (office supplies, telephone, etc.) expenses be?

_____

_____

What and how much will my variable expenses (materials, etc.) be?

_____

_____

How much will typically be left over as my salary and profit?

_____

_____

How much will I take out as a salary or reinvest into the business?

_____

_____

Income Reporter

Date	Cash/Check	For	From	Amount

Expense Reporter

Date	Cash/Check	For	From	Amount

Cash Flow Reporter

DATE:

FOR TIME PERIOD:

INCOME	Date:		Date:		Date:	
	Estimate	Actual	Estimate	Actual	Estimate	Actual
Opening Balance						
TOTAL INCOME						

EXPENSES

TOTAL EXPENSES	
Ending Balance	
Less Minimum Balance	
CASH AVAILABLE	

NOTES:

Inventory Reporter

Location:

Item #	Quantity	Description	Price	Total

TOTAL

Priced by:

Checked by:

Invoice

Invoice:	P.O. #:	Date:	Sales Rep:

Sold to:	Ship to:

Qty.	Description	Price	Total

Notes:

Subtotal	
Sales Tax	
Total	

Index